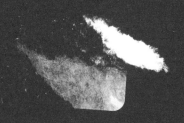

SYMBOLS OF THE OCCULT

First published in the United Kingdom in 2021 by
Thames & Hudson Ltd, 181A High Holborn,
London WC1V 7QX

Reprinted 2022, 2023

Conceived, designed and produced by
The Bright Press, an imprint of the Quarto Group,
1 Triptych Place, London
SE1 9SH, United Kingdom
T (0)20 7700 6700
www.quarto.com

Publisher: James Evans
Editorial Director: Isheeta Mustafi
Art Director: James Lawrence
Managing Editor: Jacqui Sayers
Development Editor: Abbie Sharman
Project Managers: Abbie Sharman and Stephen Haynes
Design: Studio Noel
Illustrations: John Woodcock

British Library Cataloguing-in-Publication Data
A catalogue record for this book is available from the British Library

ISBN: 978-0-500-02403-4

Printed and bound in China

Be the first to know about our new releases,
exclusive content and author events by visiting
thamesandhudson.com
thamesandhudsonusa.com
thamesandhudson.com.au

SYMBOLS
OF THE
OCCULT

A Directory of over 500 Signs, Symbols and Icons

ERIC CHALINE

CONTENTS

Foreword by Mark Stavish   6
Introduction   7

ASTROLOGY   8
Introduction   10
The Planets   12
The Zodiac   14
Zodiacal Man   18
Casting a Natal Horoscope   20
Egyptian Astrology   22
Hindu Astrology   24
The Chinese Zodiac   26
The Maya Calendar   30

THE NATURAL WORLD   32
Introduction   34
The Classical Elements   36
Chinese Cosmology   38
Trigrams   40
East Asian Natural Symbolism   42
Sacred Trees   46
The Wheel of the Seasons   48
Ogham Tree Alphabet   50
Native American Medicine Wheel   52
Four Winds & Twelve Totems   54
Australian Aboriginal Dreaming   56
Divination Stones   58
Polynesian Symbols   62
Indian Subtle Anatomy   66
Vodou Vèvè   70
Mexica Gods   72

SACRED WRITINGS   76
Introduction   78
Cuneiform   80
The Cuneiform Script   82
Mesopotamian Civilization   84
Egyptian Hieroglyphs   86
Minoan Pictograms (Phaistos Disc)   90
Ancient Greek Alphabet & Numerals   94
Celtic Symbols & Knots   98
Anglo-Saxon Runes   100
Icelandic Staves   102
Adinkra   104
Chinese Oracle Bone Script   108
Rongorongo   112
Maya Glyphs   116

OCCULT SCIENCES   120
Introduction   122
Alchemy   124
Chinese Alchemy   126
Indian Alchemy   127
Islamic Alchemy   128
Medieval & Renaissance Alchemy   130
The Four Classical Elements   132
Tria Prima   133

The Planetary Metals   134
The Mundane Elements   136
Alchemical Compounds & Units   138
Magnum Opus & the
    Philosopher's Stone   140
Other Alchemical Symbols   142
Numerology   144
Isopsephy & Gematria   146
Lucky & Unlucky Numbers   148
Sacred Geometry   152
Tetractys   154
Platonic Solids   155
Mandalas & Yantras   156
Feng Shui Luopan   160
Tiantan   161

WHITE MAGIC
& CARTOMANCY   162
Introduction   164
The Theban Alphabet   166
Scripts from *De Occulta Philosophia*   170
Malachim   172
Passing of the River   176
Celestial   178
Enochian   180
Sator Square   184
Amulets   185

Sigils   186
Planetary Seals   188
Sigils of the Archangels   190
Sigillum Dei   192
Seal of Solomon   193
Cartomancy   194
Tarot Major Arcana   196
French Playing Cards   199

BLACK MAGIC
& DEMONOLOGY   202
Introduction   204
Ahriman & Set   206
Personifications of Evil   208
Baphomet & the Templars   210
Grimoires   212
Les Douze Anneaux   214
Le Grand Grimoire   216
Ars Goetia Demonic Sigils   220

WESTERN ESOTERIC
TRADITION   226
Introduction   228
Kabbalah, Cabala, Qabalah   230
Sefirot   232
Secret Societies   234
Occult Orders   240
The New Age   248

Index   254
About the Author & Image Credits   256

FOREWORD

Symbols are humanity's earliest form of communication. In fact, it can easily be said that all forms of communication are in some manner symbolic. To understand symbols only as tools of communication and control, we would only see one small fragment of their reflection. This book will help reveal the often hidden meanings behind some of the world's most intriguing symbols.

Among the oldest forms of writing, ideograms are easily recognized literal representations of an idea but they are often too complex for daily communication, which has led to the creation of alphabets. Both communicate an idea in the mind of their user and are types of symbols. However, there is so much more to symbols than this basic understanding and it is these deeper, often hidden or secret, meanings that have led to centuries of study into the nature and use of symbols.

The human desires to understand the objective physical world and the subjective interior worlds composed of dreams, visions and psychic states have always existed in parallel. Just as awareness leads to some form of specific knowledge, so does knowledge lead to its expression. These perceptions have given rise to all of the world's philosophical (and with that, political and economic) systems. They have also given rise to schools of thought and practice hidden in the shadows of daily life and history. While the civilizations of the classical world established and maintained a host of 'mystery schools' and sects for the exploration and perpetuation of various expressions of 'secret knowledge', much of this knowledge was lost after the collapse of the Roman Empire, only to be rediscovered during the Renaissance.

The occult sciences of astrology, alchemy, ritual magic and kabbalah have some of the most notable examples of hidden meaning within symbols. They have often, out of necessity and tradition, existed in semi-secret across the centuries. To understand the symbols associated with the occult sciences, it is important to explore the context in which they existed side by side and the highly hostile political and ecclesiastical environments they experienced at times, which led to their knowledge being hidden and them becoming more occult. This 're-veiling' or hiding of ancient wisdom and its means of being directly experienced on an individual level primarily took place in plain sight. That is, through the use of symbols.

To explore the use of symbols is to plunge to the depths of our being and take note of the practical and well-designed manipulation of the powers of the human mind: primarily those of memory and phantasy or imagination.

Mark Stavish – Founder and Director of Studies at the Institute for Hermetic Studies

INTRODUCTION

Confronted by a vast, baffling universe, our ancestors divined occult patterns in the heavens and the natural world that, long before religion or science, gave them meaning, purpose and agency. The symbols featured in this book's seven chapters represent the ways humanity has expressed and controlled its relationship with the occult over the past several thousand years. The survival of occult symbolism through succeeding ages of faith and reason speaks of its enduring significance and power and of our deep need for the reassurance it can provide.

We interact with the world through symbols: when we want to know the time, we don't look up at the sky but at numbers on a digital display; when we communicate with others, we often prefer to use text or, increasingly, emojis. For some cognitive scientists, it is our facility with signs, symbols, letters and numbers that makes us truly human, rather than the ability to use language and tools, which other animals are also known to possess. Only we have the unique ability, through the creation and manipulation of abstract symbols, to make the intuitive and counterintuitive associations that allow us to understand and, ultimately, to control and transform the world.

Imagine the smiths of the distant past, who extracted metals from ores and cast them into objects both sacred and profane. As is often the case, they remembered the one time out of a hundred when the process worked perfectly, but not knowing why, they ascribed their success to whatever rituals they had performed as they worked – of such things is magic made. Apply this principle to all human activities and technologies, from farming and hunting to ceramics, metallurgy and medicine, and you can see how the occult became incorporated into every aspect of daily life.

Move forward to the invention of writing, and invocations, spells and rituals were recorded to be passed down to others or made into talismans to protect or curse the living and the dead. For most of history, occult knowledge was thought too precious and dangerous to be shared with everyone; thus, it was encoded in secret alphabets of signs and symbols that only initiates could understand. These mysterious symbols have endured to the present day to intrigue, charm, reassure and entertain us.

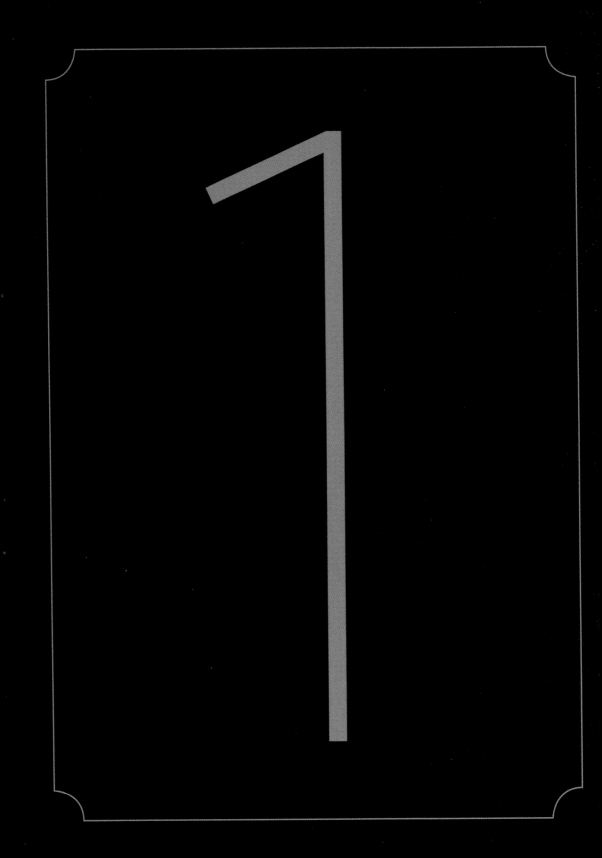

ASTROLOGY

Astrology rightly takes its place as the opening topic of this book, because it was the pre-eminent occult science that gave our ancestors a sense of who they were and what the future might hold, providing them with a degree of certainty in a dangerous, unpredictable world.

The occult may well have begun when our ancestors looked up at the stars and asked, 'What are we and how do we fit into this vast cosmological machine?' Natal and divinatory astrology is the one surviving occult science that continues to guide, reassure and entertain us today. But not all cultures have sought answers in the stars: several looked to time's repeating cycles as the true guides to a person's character and fate.

From the point of view of our ancestors, the heavenly bodies rotated around them on Earth. The Sun and Moon, being apparently the largest, were for several ancient peoples their most important gods, but this was not always the case. In the Greco-Roman pantheon, the sun god Apollo (Helios) and his sister, the moon goddess Artemis (Diana), were major divinities in their own right, but they were the children of the king of the gods, Zeus (Jupiter or Jove). Like their father, their siblings Hermes (Mercury), Aphrodite (Venus) and Ares (Mars), and their grandfather Chronos (Saturn), they are tiny pinpricks of light in the vast canvas of the night sky. How do we explain the apparent mismatch between size and astrological significance?

Despite its importance in our daily lives, the Sun disappears every night and weakens and strengthens with the seasons, while the Moon waxes and wanes during its cycle, also doomed to almost vanish every month. Both are subject to regular eclipses, leading to fears that they have been 'eaten' or 'died', never to return. The planets on the other hand, moving against the backdrop of the zodiacal constellations, reappear undiminished every night, regardless of time or season. As the fixed constituents of a cosmos in a constant state of flux, they seemed dependable and trustworthy, which may explain why they, and not just the Sun and Moon, were considered to possess major astrological influence.

The ancient Chinese and the Maya, who were highly skilled astronomers, took another approach to natal divination. They did not look to Sun, Moon, planets and stars and their positions on an astrological chart to predict the future. Instead, they used their observations of the heavens to create highly accurate calendars that allowed them to measure cycles of different lengths, and they then assigned divinatory meanings to the hour, day, week, month and year of an individual's birth.

A map of the geocentric (Earth-centred) cosmos, from the star atlas Harmonia Macrocosmica by Andreas Cellarius (1660).

SUN

MOON

MERCURY

VENUS

MARS

JUPITER

SATURN

NEPTUNE

URANUS

THE PLANETS

Astrology was based on a geocentric (Earth-centred) model of the cosmos in which the seven classical planets – the Sun, Moon, Mercury, Venus, Mars, Jupiter and Saturn – were believed to orbit the Earth. Astrology had to adapt to the heliocentric (Sun-centred) solar system described by Nicolaus Copernicus in the sixteenth century, and find roles for two new planets, Uranus and Neptune, and also – for seventy-five years – Pluto, until it was demoted to the ranks of the 'dwarf planets'.

SUN

The Sun indicates the 'star' sign on a natal horoscope. It is associated with the sun gods Helios and Apollo. It is represented by a simple circle with a dot in the centre.

MOON

The Moon represents the shifting nature of a person's emotional intelligence, associated with the goddess Artemis (Diana). It is most often depicted in crescent form.

MERCURY

Mercury is the planet of communication and intelligence, associated with the god Hermes (Mercury). It is said to illustrate the winged cap and caduceus of the Greek god.

VENUS

Venus is the planet of beauty, love, sex and the feminine principle, represented by the goddess Aphrodite (Venus).

MARS

Mars is the planet of action, motivation and the masculine principle, represented by the god Ares (Mars). His shield and spear make up the elements of this symbol.

JUPITER

Jupiter is the planet of material expansion and prosperity, represented by the father of the gods, Zeus (Jupiter or Jove). This symbol could represent Jupiter's thunderbolt or his bird, an eagle. However, it could also stand for the letter Z in honour of Zeus, Jupiter's Greek counterpart.

SATURN

Saturn is the planet of order and chaos, of organization and structure, represented by the titan Chronos (Saturn). This symbol shows Saturn's sickle. Saturn was the Roman god of agriculture.

NEPTUNE

Neptune, discovered in 1846, is the planet of illusion, dreams and fantasy, represented by the god of the sea, Poseidon (Neptune). The symbol itself is his trident.

URANUS

Uranus, discovered in 1781, is the planet of rebellion and innovation, represented by the titan Ouranos. The H in this symbol is taken from the surname of its discoverer (Herschel) and the circle depicts the Sun.

THE ZODIAC

The night sky of the pre-industrial ancestors of the West was a brilliant tapestry of Moon, planets and stars, and the Milky Way, a cloud-like ribbon of stars that forms part of our galaxy. Finding patterns within this apparent chaos, they identified the figures of real or mythological animals, objects and supernatural beings, creating twelve star groupings known as the zodiacal constellations.

Even those who might claim to know nothing about astronomy will be able to name at least one constellation or maybe several, because most of us know our astrological Sun, or birth, sign. Each one corresponds to one of the twelve constellations of the Greco-Babylonian zodiac, themselves part of the forty-eight constellations described by the astronomer Ptolemy, who was born in Roman Egypt, around 100 CE.

The twelve zodiacal constellations consist of stars that are visible to the naked eye (since there were no telescopes before the early seventeenth century), but they have no relationship to one another apart from those imagined by ancient astronomers and astrologers. For example, Taurus looks like a crooked letter Y with a spur coming out of the right-hand branch, or 'horn', made up of a dozen or so stars. And yet the choice of the bull for this group of disparate stars is not as random as it might appear. As a springtime constellation, the appearance of Taurus was an important marker in the agricultural year. Likewise, its association with the bull speaks of its importance to Western ancestors for whom cattle were important symbols of power and fertility, evidence of wealth, status and power, as well as manifestations of the divine and the supernatural.

In astrology, the zodiacal constellations each occupy thirty degrees of the sky, making twelve signs of equal extent, but this is only a convention, as the real constellations remain in view for varying lengths of time. Another thing to take into account is the precession of the equinoxes (the shift in the Earth's axis relative to the Sun and stars) over the past few thousand years, which means that the actual positions of the constellations are out of synch with the zodiac. So you may think you are an Aries, but, depending on whereabouts in that sign you were born, you might actually be a Pisces.

ARIES (THE RAM)

Aries is represented by a pair of curled ram's horns. As the second animal species to be domesticated, sheep play a crucial role in human civilization. In ancient Mesopotamia, rams' horns were a symbol of divinity, and the Egyptian sun god Amun-Ra is also represented as a ram.

TAURUS (THE BULL)

The horned circle is similar to the modern Wicca symbol for the 'horned god'. As one of the most important animals for pastoralists and settled farmers, it is unsurprising that the bull should feature in the zodiac. Associated divinities include the Egyptian gods Hathor and Apis.

GEMINI (THE TWINS)

The symbol for Gemini resembles the number two in Roman numerals and is also reminiscent of the constellation Gemini, which resembles two stick figures holding hands. The sign is associated with the Dioscuri, the twins Castor and Pollux, the former mortal and the latter immortal.

CANCER (THE CRAB)

The symbol for Cancer resembles a pair of sixes top-and-tailed and lying on their sides, which could represent the claws of a crab or crayfish. In legend, the Greek goddess Hera (Juno) placed the crab in the heavens after it had been crushed underfoot by Herakles (Hercules).

LEO (THE LION)

In its outline, the large, bright constellation of Leo was thought to resemble the Nemean Lion with which it is associated. Zeus (Jupiter) placed this lion in the heavens to commemorate the labours of his son, the demigod Herakles (Hercules).

VIRGO (THE VIRGIN)

It is unclear why Virgo is represented by an M with an inward loop, but it has been suggested that this represents the chastity of the mythological maidens associated with the sign, in opposition to the more phallic tail added to the M of Scorpio.

LIBRA (THE SCALES)

Libra is the only inanimate object in the zodiac. Its symbol is a stylized balance, which is associated with justice in ancient Egyptian and Greco-Roman iconography. The sign used to correspond to the autumnal equinox, when night and day are equal.

SCORPIO (THE SCORPION)

Scorpio's sign is an M with a perky tail that alludes to the scorpion's famous 'sting in the tail' and the supposed sexual prowess of people born under the sign. It takes the Sun only six days to transit the constellation Scorpio, making it the shortest zodiacal sign.

SAGITTARIUS (THE ARCHER)

Sagittarius is one of two constellations associated with the centaur, the half-man half-horse creature of Greco-Roman myth. *Sagitta* means 'arrow' in Latin – hence the symbol – but part of the constellation is now known unceremoniously as the 'teapot'.

CAPRICORN (THE GOAT)

The inverted triangle of Capricorn vaguely resembles a pictographic representation of the horns of a goat. The earlier Babylonian sign for this constellation represented the god Ea, who was imagined as a hybrid of human, goat and fish.

AQUARIUS (THE WATER CARRIER)

Although the sign is represented as two wavy lines – suggesting water or the ocean – Aquarius is an air sign. It is also associated with the god Ea, who brought life-giving rain to the parched deserts of Mesopotamia.

PISCES (THE FISH)

The quintessential water sign, Pisces is associated with the goddess Aphrodite (Venus) and her son Eros (Cupid), who, chased by the monster Typhon, dived into the river Euphrates and either transformed into fish, or were taken to safety by two fish.

ZODIACAL MAN

In medieval and Renaissance Europe, medicine combined astrology with the theory of the four bodily humours, or humourism, inherited from ancient Greek and Roman medical practice. The signs of the zodiac corresponded to different parts of the body and their associated organs and functions. Hence, the medieval physician needed to combine the roles of healer and astrologer in order to diagnose and treat his patients.

The maxim 'as above, so below' was a guiding principle of pre-modern European thought (a part of the tradition known as Hermeticism) that saw humans as subject to the influences of the heavens – notably of the positions and movements of the Sun, Moon and stars, which were believed to be attached to spheres rotating around the Earth. In this Earth-centred cosmos, astrology was used to divine an individual's character, their future, and, in the case of illness, to diagnose the causes of disease and determine how and when they should be treated.

Each sign was associated with a different part of the body and its related organs and physiological functions: Aries with the head, eyes and adrenal glands; Taurus with the neck, throat and ears; Gemini with the shoulders, lungs and arms; Cancer with the chest, breasts and several minor internal organs; Leo with the sides, upper back, spleen and heart; Virgo with the abdomen, liver and intestines; Libra with the hips, buttocks, lower back and kidneys; Scorpio with the sexual organs, pelvis, bladder and rectum; Sagittarius with the thighs, legs and groin; Capricorn with the knees, bone, skin and nerves; Aquarius with the lower legs and blood circulation; and Pisces with the feet.

Medieval physicians combined zodiacal anatomy with ancient Greek notions of physiology that held that diseases were caused by imbalances of the four humours:

blood, yellow bile, black bile and phlegm, each paired with one of the four classical elements and characterized by heat, cold, dryness and wetness (see diagram below). Once he had diagnosed the disease and identified the part of the body to be treated, the physician needed to cast a horoscope to determine the best time to perform an operation or begin a prescribed course of treatment. The cardinal rule was that treatment should not begin when the Moon was in the sign of the zodiac associated with the diseased body part.

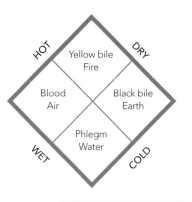

Opposite — Zodiacal human anatomy, showing the signs with their associated body parts and organs.

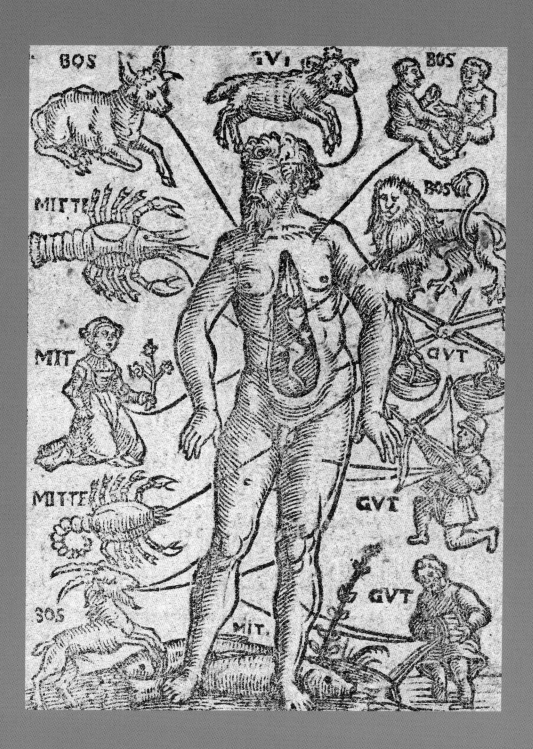

CASTING A NATAL HOROSCOPE

A Western natal horoscope, or birth chart, is a representation of the cosmos at the moment of a person's birth. The Earth is at the centre, surrounded by an outer ring inscribed with the symbols representing the signs of the zodiac named after the twelve constellations; the symbols for the Sun, Moon and planets are entered within the main body of the chart. Other significant symbols indicate the positions of the cardinal points that are used to calculate the divisions of the chart.

In order to cast a birth chart, an astrologer needs to plot the exact positions of the Sun, Moon, planets and ascendant (the sign rising on the eastern horizon) for the location, date and time of the subject's birth. A modern astrological chart is shaped like a wheel with the twelve signs of the zodiac arranged around its rim. The wheel is divided into twelve houses, whose cusps (dividing lines) radiate like spokes from the centre. The positions of the cusps are determined by the cardinal points on the circumference: the ascendant and the descendant, the midheaven and its opposite point, the *imum coeli*. The houses denote different aspects of a person's life: 1. Self, 2. Wealth, 3. Siblings, 4. Parents, 5. Children, 6. Health, 7. Spouse, 8. Death, 9. Travel, 10. Kingdom, 11. Belonging, 12. Seclusion.

The position of the Sun on the chart denotes the person's birth, or star, sign. Although in popular astrology only the star sign is considered significant, it is just one piece of information that astrologers use to interpret a chart. In addition to plotting the positions of the Sun, Moon, planets and ascendant within the zodiac signs and houses, they have to interpret their positive and negative aspects (relative positions) to one another and to the ascendant and the other important points on the circumference.

A person's star sign denotes their nature, while the ascendant sign represents the effects of nurture.

The older style of natal chart pictured opposite (below) is the birth chart of King Charles I of England (born on 19 November 1600). The houses are represented as twelve interlocking triangles around the square containing the king's name, date and time of birth and the latitude of his place of birth. The zodiacal symbols are placed within the houses with numerals indicating their astronomical positions.

Top — A modern astrological chart showing the twelve signs of the zodiac.

Below — This style of natal horoscope, favoured in the medieval period and later, carries the same information as a circular chart but in a different format.

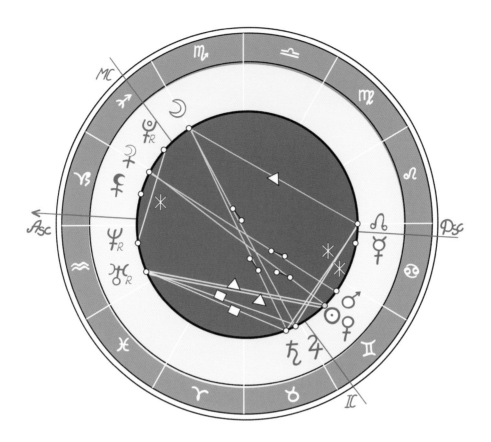

EGYPTIAN ASTROLOGY

The Egyptian system of natal and divinatory astrology has close links with Greco-Babylonian astrology, which was introduced into Egypt in the fourth century BCE. Fusing two ancient traditions, it features additions and refinements, several of which predate the arrival of the Greeks in Egypt. The study of the heavens is attested in the earliest dynastic periods of ancient Egypt, and the use of symbols representing the Sun, Moon, planets and constellations in tombs and on the inside of coffin lids dates back to the third millennium BCE.

In the fourth century BCE, the Macedonians conquered the Persian Empire, which included modern-day Egypt, Iraq, Iran, Central Asia, Pakistan and northern India. They took with them the Greco-Babylonian astrological tradition, introducing it to their conquests, where it was adapted for local use and fused with local astrological and divinatory practices. Hermes Trismegistus, a legendary author of early texts on astrology and alchemy, is closely associated with the Egyptian god of wisdom, knowledge and writing, Thoth – leading some scholars to claim that the origins of astrology are to be found in ancient Egypt and not in Babylon. What is beyond doubt is that the astronomical and astrological traditions of Egypt are extremely ancient, as attested by symbols representing the thirty-six decans (star groupings); their presence on the inside of tenth-dynasty coffin lids (c. 2100 BCE) indicates their use as powerful magical talismans intended to protect and guide the deceased during their journey through the underworld.

After the introduction of Greco-Babylonian astrology, the decans became part of a syncretic astrological system, blending elements of different beliefs, that was used into the Islamic period and later reintroduced to western Europe via Arabic treatises. The decans were associated with the gods and were used to measure the hours of the day, as well as the ten-day periods making up one Egyptian year. Each zodiacal sign was divided into three decans, giving its three 'phases' that were used in religious rituals and in the manufacture of talismans to cure diseases.

The ceiling of the Temple of Dendera, shown opposite, illustrates the fusion of Egyptian and Greco-Babylonian astrology. The Egyptians replaced the Greco-Babylonian zodiacal signs with Egyptian deities: the Nile (Capricorn), Amon-Ra (Taurus), Mut (Scorpio), Geb (Aquarius), Osiris (Aries), Isis (Pisces), Thoth (Virgo), Horus (Libra), Anubis (Leo), Seth (Gemini), Bastet (Cancer) and Sekhmet (Sagittarius).

The ceiling of the Temple of Dendera, showing the Egyptian zodiac, which replaces the earlier signs with Egyptian divinities.

HINDU ASTROLOGY

Hindu astrology, or *Jyotisha*, is a syncretic system that fuses the Greco-Babylonian tradition, transmitted to the Indian subcontinent by the conquests of Alexander the Great in the fourth century BCE, with ancient Vedic astronomical observations that were used to determine the most propitious times for sacrificial rituals to honour the gods. Although there are many similarities between the Western and Indian astrological traditions, there are also many differences that have accrued over the past two millennia of separate development and practice.

The most striking difference between Western and Hindu astrology is that an individual's birth sign, as determined by Western astrology, will be different from the same person's sign according to Jyotisha. Western astrology determines a person's birth sign by calculating the position of the Sun relative to a moving zodiac, while Indian astrology uses a fixed zodiac. Because of an astronomical phenomenon known as the precession of the equinoxes, the two systems are now out of synch by twenty-two degrees of the ecliptic (a whole astrological sign is thirty degrees), meaning that if you read the horoscope for Taurus in your daily paper – unless you were born towards the end of that sign – then according to Jyotisha you should be reading the horoscope for Aries instead.

Jyotisha shares the basic elements of Western astrology, including the twelve signs, or *Rashi: Meṣa* मेष (Aries), *Vṛṣabha* वृषभ (Taurus), *Mithuna* मिथुन (Gemini), *Karka* कर्क (Cancer), *Siṃha* सिंह (Leo), *Kanyā* कन्या (Virgo), *Tulā* तुला (Libra), *Vṛścika* वृश्चिक (Scorpio), *Dhanuṣa* धनुष (Sagittarius), *Makara* मकर (Capricorn), *Kumbha* कुंभ (Aquarius) and *Mīna* मीन (Pisces) and the houses, or *Bhava*. The influence of the Sun, Moon and planets, collectively known as the *Navagraha*, varies according to their positions, transits, conjunctions and aspects, but Jyotisha adds two shadow bodies or planets, *Rahu* and *Ketu*. Other significant differences include the use of the planetary periods, or *Dasha*, which govern the state of being of a person and of the 27 lunar mansions, or *Nakshatra*, which each cover 13° 20′ of the celestial sphere and which are used to determine auspicious and inauspicious days in predictive astrology. A final significant difference between Hindu and Western astrology is the former's integration into the Hindu belief system, notably with the concepts of karma and reincarnation.

A depiction of the Indian zodiac. Although the signs have a distinctive Indian flavour, they are recognizably similar to those used in the West.

THE CHINESE ZODIAC

Although the Chinese zodiac bears a superficial resemblance to its Western counterpart – they are both divided into twelve signs – the two systems depend on completely different belief systems and methodologies to ascertain the characteristics of a person born under an astronomical sign and to predict the course of their future life. Instead of using abstract symbols, Chinese diviners use animals as mnemonic devices for complex cosmological concepts.

There have been commercial, scientific and cultural exchanges between China, India and the Near East along the Silk Route since antiquity. Although Indian astrological texts were translated into Chinese in the early centuries CE, neither Greco-Babylonian nor Indian astrology was adopted by the Chinese, who, however, enthusiastically embraced Indian Buddhism. How can we explain these choices on the part of the subjects of the Chinese empire? It could be that its ancient, well-established zodiacal system was so well integrated with Chinese Taoist beliefs and practices – such as geomancy and other forms of divination, ancestor worship and medicine – that it easily resisted the challenge from a rival form of astrology, based on a radically different conception of the cosmos and humanity's place within it.

As we shall see in the next chapter, the ancient Chinese believed that the cosmos was in a constant state of flux, driven by the interplay of yin and yang with the *wuxing*, or five elements. They applied this to the macrocosm of the universe and the microcosm of the body. Chinese astronomers and sages studied the movement of astronomical bodies and the passage of the seasons to discern the cycles that governed every aspect of existence. Every year in a repeating cycle, every month, week, day or hour was subject to the complex interplay of yin–yang and the wuxing. They encoded this knowledge into a lunar calendar that they used to determine a person's character and predict the course of future events.

In the popular version of the Chinese zodiac, only the sign corresponding to the birth year is used, but professional diviners have to take into account the month, day and hour of a person's birth, because each is ruled by different animals known as the 'inner,' 'true' and 'secret' animals. A true understanding of a person's character and future can only be discerned by understanding the positive and negative aspects of the relationships between the animals representing these four times.

The Chinese zodiac superficially resembles the Western version, but the signs correspond to temporal periods – years, weeks, days, hours – rather than astronomical bodies.

Each of the twelve signs of the Chinese zodiac is associated with either yin or yang, one of the wuxing, and a two-hour period of the day. Their association with animals does not imply a direct equation of the signs with the characteristics of living creatures; rather it is a metaphorical description that acts as a mnemonic for the abstract concepts the signs represent. Note that Chinese animal symbolism is very different from that of Western and Near-Eastern cultures that see certain animals, such as the pig, snake or rat, as ritually unclean, unhygienic or evil.

RAT（鼠）

Yang; element: water; time of day:
11.00 p.m.–1.00 a.m. The pictogram shows
the animal's head and whiskers. Rats are
commonly eaten in some places, but are
also known to carry bubonic plague.

OX（牛）

Yin; element: earth; time of day:
1.00–3.00 a.m. An important agricultural
symbol, the ox was said to hear with its nose.
A 'spring ox' made of clay is broken with
sticks to represent the rebirth of nature.

TIGER（虎）

Yang; element: wood; time of day:
3.00–5.00 a.m. In China, the tiger, not the
lion, is the 'king of the jungle'. The character's
two elements represent its stripes and its
ability to stand on its hind legs.

RABBIT（兔）

Yin; element: wood; time of day:
5.00–7.00 a.m. In contrast with its Western
association with constant rutting, the rabbit is
associated with mercy, elegance and beauty.
It is considered the luckiest sign
of the Chinese zodiac.

DRAGON（龙）

Yang; element: earth; time of day:
7.00–9.00 a.m. Unlike its destructive
Western counterpart, the Chinese dragon is
associated with good luck and health. A sign
of power and authority, it was embroidered
on the emperor's 'dragon robe'.

SNAKE（蛇）

Yin; element: fire; time of day:
9.00–11.00 a.m. In certain aspects, snakes
are considered evil but in others they are
deemed to be lucky because of their kinship
with dragons. The character for 'snake' is said
to represent a standing cobra.

HORSE (马)

Yang; element: fire; time of day: 11.00 a.m.–1.00 p.m. The character for 'horse' represents its head, mane and legs. The sleeves and queue that characterized the official dress of Qing officials were inspired by a horse's hooves and tail.

GOAT (OR SHEEP) (羊)

Yin; element: earth; time of day: 1.00–3.00 p.m. The character for 'sheep' shows its horns and four legs seen from above. The sign symbolizes filial piety and is the emblem of a retired life. It was one of the six sacrificial animals.

MONKEY (猴)

Yang; element: metal; time of day: 3.00–5.00 p.m. Though the monkey is a symbol of ugliness and trickery, the Monkey King in *Journey to the West* ensures the introduction of Buddhism to China by helping the monk Tripitaka.

ROOSTER (鸡)

Yin; element: metal; time of day: 5.00–7.00 p.m. The quintessential 'king of the roost', the cockerel is a symbol of both pride and leadership. As in the West, it is associated with the early hours of the day, which traditionally begins at 'cockcrow'.

DOG (狗)

Yang; element: earth; time of day: 7.00–9.00 p.m. Dogs have a chequered reputation in Chinese symbolism, standing for both protectors and scavengers. They were formerly bred as imperial pets and also for their pelts and meat.

PIG (猪)

Yin; element: water; time of day: 9.00–11.00 p.m. The pig was once a sacrificial animal. Pork meat can be infected with dangerous pathogens, and the Chinese invoked the God of Swine to protect themselves from disease.

THE MAYA CALENDAR

The pre-Columbian Native American cultures of Mesoamerica, including the Olmecs, Toltecs, Maya and Aztecs, developed advanced mathematics and astronomy for the purposes of ritual, astrology and divination. The classic Maya (third to tenth centuries CE) were the most advanced mathematicians and astronomers of the ancient world, who created an astronomical calendrical system that was unrivalled until the modern period.

The Maya lived in an area that spans southern Mexico, Guatemala, Belize, Honduras and El Salvador. During the classic period, they built vast cities and ceremonial centres on the Yucatán peninsula, which they mysteriously abandoned in the tenth century, moving north to build new cities that endured until the arrival of the Spanish conquistadors in the sixteenth century.

When the 'lost' Maya sites were rediscovered by Westerners during the nineteenth century, much was made of the superficial similarities between Maya glyphs and Egyptian hieroglyphs, and between Maya pyramids and Mesopotamian ziggurats. Quite apart from the vast distance between Mesoamerica and the Near East, as well as the mismatch in time between the flowering of these very different cultures, there is no evidence in contemporary documents or the archaeological record that establishes any links between the Old and New Worlds. The extraordinary achievements of the Maya in mathematics and astronomy, which allowed them to create the ancient world's most complex and accurate calendar, are entirely due to their patient observations of the heavens over many centuries.

We shall discover the magical and divinatory symbols of the Maya calendar in Chapter 3, but here we must mention the Maya's unique view of time that led them to create a calendrical system that combined the 260-day ritual *Tzolk'in* calendar with the 365-day *Haab'* solar calendar, allowing them to calculate dates in the distant future and predict eclipses, planetary transits and the passage of comets, with an accuracy not rivalled until modern times. The Maya saw time as cyclical, believing that events that had happened in the past would reoccur in the future. They compiled vast libraries of books of divination that recorded past events, calibrating them with their astronomical observations, so that they could predict what would happen in the near or distant future. They applied this to the character and life course of a person born on a certain day in the current calendrical cycle.

The three interlocking wheels of the Maya calendar: the numbers one to thirteen, the 260 days of the Tzolk'in and the 365 days of the Haab'.

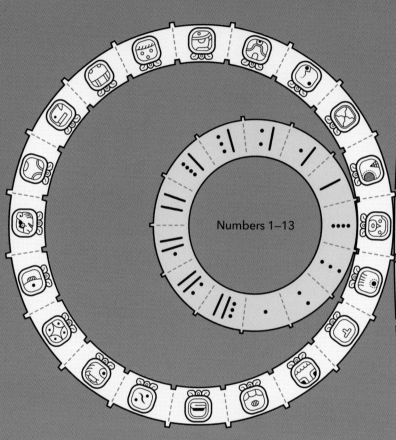
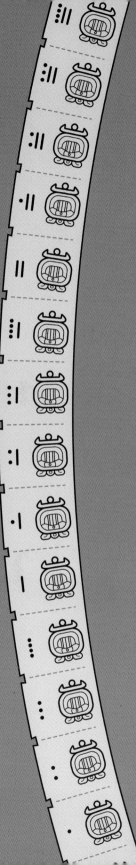

365 days of the Haab'

Numbers 1–13

260 days of the Tzolk'in

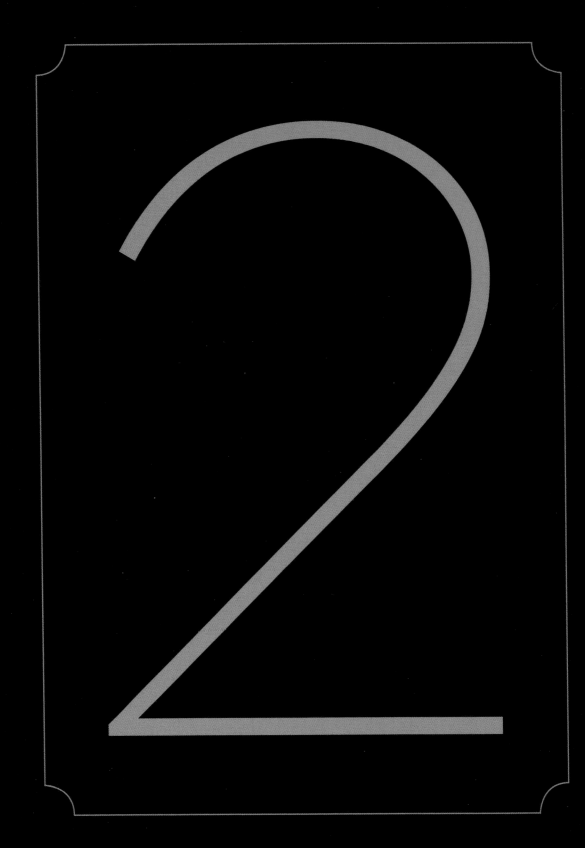

THE NATURAL WORLD

We do not know exactly when modern humans first left
their African home and set out into the unknown. They
travelled with the most basic toolkit, but they must have
possessed an intelligence that enabled them to thrive
in hostile and unpredictable environments. Perhaps
they already believed that they could, to some degree,
understand and even influence the new worlds that
lay before them.

At 300,000 to 350,000 years old, *Homo sapiens* is a young species when compared to the emergence of life on planet Earth between 4.5 and 3.5 billion years BP (before present). But what is even more recent is the emergence of traits and abilities that together signal our species' attainment of 'behavioural modernity', which include art, burial customs, religion and, as has been argued, magical thinking and symbolic reasoning through which humans sought to understand and influence the natural world.

Picture a group of Stone Age hunters entering a cave, torches in hand, and descending to its deepest chambers, whose walls are covered in depictions of prey species, where the shaman and elders of the tribe have prepared the magical rituals that will ensure the success of the forthcoming hunt. Like later peoples who lived in harmony with the natural world, they identified with different animals and plants in relationships that claimed direct kinship and imposed obligations that anthropologists have explained with the concepts of 'totem' and 'taboo', whereby a group of people ask permission to hunt an animal species that they identify with and obtain absolution for the lives they are about to take.

This reconstruction is only a guess, but not an outlandish one, considering how humans in historical times have sought to control the natural world through magic. Prehistoric art includes abstract symbols and handprints, whose exact meaning is unknown, but its representations of the animals Western ancestors depended on for their survival are extraordinary in their sophistication. Hence, at this stage, animals and their depictions are one, without the need for abstract symbols but prefiguring them in their ritual uses.

There is something quite wondrous about the magical thinking of Western ancestors, which differs from religious thinking in a very important way: while, in religion, humans are the passive recipients of divine favour or punishment, in magic they set themselves up as the equals of the forces they are trying to control, be it their animal prey species, the plants they harvest or the natural phenomena they may be subject to. As humans deepened their questioning of the natural world, to discover new ways to understand it, they created ever more abstract symbols to describe its constituents and processes.

Stone age painting of a steppe bison from the Altamira Cave in Cantabria, Spain.

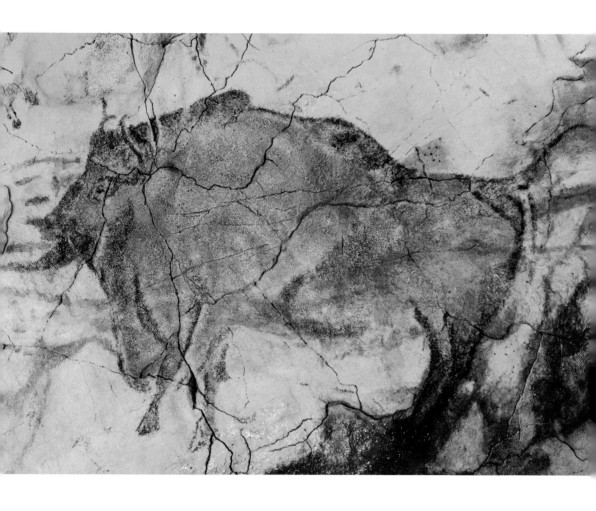

THE CLASSICAL ELEMENTS

With the symbols for the classical elements, fire, earth, air and water – to which the Greek philosopher and natural scientist Aristotle added a fifth, aether – we begin the exploration of the Western world's early attempts to understand the composition of physical matter. During the medieval period, the doctrine of the elements was the foundation of the pseudoscience of alchemy; this in turn became the basis for the science of chemistry, which, at the last count, has identified 118 chemical elements that constitute the periodic table.

The concept of four or five elements has existed in many cultures, but in the West it was the ancient Greeks who proposed the first rational explanation of the composition of matter. Greek philosophers drew on observation and experiment to hypothesize that all matter was made up of the four elements of fire, earth, air and water. Aristotle's aether was the incorruptible constituent of the heavens, exempt from the processes of creation, transmutation and decay. This theory remained central to the understanding of physical matter until the Renaissance and was a basic principle of medieval alchemy, astrology and humourism (the study of the four bodily humours).

In astrological lore, each sign was classed as having the qualities of one of the four elements; for example, Aries, Leo and Sagittarius were said to be fire signs. This classification, along with an association with the four seasons, was used to explain the basic nature of a given sign. The water signs, Cancer, Scorpio and Pisces, were cold and wet through their association with winter. However, each sign occurred in more than one season, and this changed their elemental qualities. For example, Aries, being a fire and a spring sign, was both hot and dry, and hot and wet.

Medieval physicians made similar associations between the four elements and the four humours of the body (see diagram below and page 18). Yellow bile was paired with fire, black bile with earth, blood with air and phlegm with water. The humours were further characterized as being hot or cold and wet or dry. These associations connected the system of elemental and seasonal characteristics to the signs of the zodiac in a closed pseudoscientific belief system, in which belief in one constituent reinforced belief in the others, despite there being absolutely no evidence for their existence or practical efficacy.

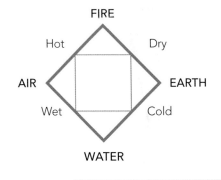

The elements and the four humoural qualities.

These symbols for the elements are derived from the diagram opposite, which shows the relationship between the elements and their properties.

FIRE

Associated with the signs Aries, Leo and Sagittarius.

EARTH

Associated with the signs Taurus, Virgo and Capricorn.

AIR

Associated with the signs Gemini, Libra and Aquarius.

WATER

Associated with the signs Cancer, Scorpio and Pisces.

AETHER

Incorruptible element that makes up the heavens and heavenly bodies.

CHINESE COSMOLOGY

The wuxing, the five phases of matter and energy, yin and yang, *qi* and the *bagua* (eight trigrams) represent the basic elements of Chinese cosmology, which remains extremely influential in mainland China and the large communities of the Chinese diaspora. This holds that the cosmos is in constant motion, mobilized by the complementary paired opposites yin and yang and animated by the subtle energy qi, which together transmute the five phases of wood, fire, earth, metal and water. The wuxing are used in medicine, geomancy and the divinatory method using the bagua laid out in the classic divinatory text, *I Ching*, the Book of Changes (see page 40).

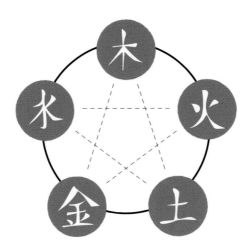

WUXING

The wuxing are not equivalent to the ancient Greek elements of earth, air, fire, water and aether, or to the modern scientific chemical elements, both of which represent the fixed components of physical matter. Rather, they must be seen as the transitions between different phases of matter and energy. A good way to understand the differences between the two systems is that the Western elements represent states, while the wuxing represent processes. The transitions of the wuxing create the two cycles of generation (生, *sheng*): wood feeds fire, fire creates earth, earth yields metal, metal condenses water and water feeds wood; and of destruction (克, *ke*): wood splits earth, earth absorbs water, water douses fire, fire melts metal and metal chops wood.

YIN AND YANG

Dualism is at the centre of Chinese cosmology, which holds that everything in the cosmos is made up of pairs of complementary opposites – light and dark, Sun and Moon, active and passive, male and female, wet and dry, hot and cold, positive and negative – that are in a constant state of flux and transformation. Harmony and health are maintained when these opposites are in balance. This is symbolized in the *Taijitu* (太極圖) diagram, in which each half of the circle, representing yin (陰) and yang (陽), contains the seed of its opposite.

QI

The subtle energy qi has no counterpart in the Western tradition. It is the force that animates all living things. We are born with an inherited store of qi from our parents, and we acquire more from the environment, the air we breathe and the food we eat. The Chinese believe that our store of qi can be diminished by disease, which is caused by imbalances of yin and yang, but qi can also be increased and its flow around the body improved by following the correct diet, taking certain herbal preparations and performing exercises such as *qigong* and t'ai chi.

TRIGRAMS

The *bagua*, or eight trigrams, are the basis for the most ancient and authoritative book of Chinese divination, *I Ching* (translated into English as the Book of Changes), which many Chinese still use to guide every aspect of their lives. The *I Ching* was compiled in the late ninth century BCE, during the Zhou dynasty, and modern versions incorporate detailed commentaries and interpretations added during the succeeding centuries.

The first yin–yang oracles in China used wooden or stone counters, one marked with a solid line, the symbol for yang and 'yes', and the other with a broken line, the symbol for yin and 'no'. This system was too simple to answer the complex questions posed by an increasingly sophisticated urban culture, and a second line was added to create four counters: yang-yang, yin-yin, yang-yin, yin-yang. However, even this was found too simple, and a third line created the bagua, the eight trigrams, shown opposite.

In their final divinatory iteration in the *I Ching*, the trigrams were combined into pairs to produce sixty-four hexagrams. For example, *t'ai*, peace, is made up of *k'un*, the receptive, Earth, above *ch'ien*, the creative, Heaven. The hexagrams may be cast by throwing coins with one side representing yin and the other yang, or bundles of yarrow sticks, from whose patterns the hexagrams are identified. These are simple processes governed by chance, creating an occult link between chance patterns and events in the real world. The interpretation of the hexagrams is so challenging that learned commentaries on the subject occupy the bulk of the *I Ching*.

A bagua talisman made of copper, silver, bronze or jade, engraved with the trigrams arranged around a central yin–yang diagram is a good luck charm that protects the wearer

from misfortune and assures their future prosperity. The bagua can also be seen over the entrances to homes, commercial premises and Daoist temples. In feng shui (Chinese geomancy), a bagua diagram is superimposed over the floor plan of a house, shop or office, to decide how best to enhance and maintain inward flow of the subtle energy, qi, that assures both the health and the prosperity of the occupants.

A small metal bagua talisman, with a yin-yang symbol in the centre, worn for protection from bad luck.

CH'IEN

the creative, strong,
Heaven, father

K'UN

the receptive, devoted and
yielding, Earth, mother

CHEN

the arousing,
inciting movement, thunder,
eldest son

K'AN

the abysmal, dangerous,
water, second son

KEN

keeping still, resting,
mountain, third son

SUN

the gentle, penetrating,
wind and wood,
eldest daughter

LI

the clinging, light-giving,
fire, second daughter

TUI

the joyous, lake,
third daughter

EAST ASIAN
NATURAL SYMBOLISM

In the Chinese zodiac, the twelve animal symbols represent complex cosmological concepts, and an implied connection with the animal itself exists only in simple interpretations of Chinese natal divination. The Chinese transmitted these associations, evolved over millennia, throughout East Asia, where they replaced or fused with pre-existing traditions of animal and plant symbolism. This section features a selection of the most common East Asian animal and plant symbols and explores their coded meanings.

Unlike the cultures of the West and Near East that have been continuously transformed by the emergence of new religions, human migrations and other social, economic and political upheavals, China has shown remarkable linguistic, social and cultural continuity that survived even the Communist revolution. Traditional practices such as divination, the zodiac, geomancy, traditional Chinese medicine and t'ai chi, though temporarily suppressed in the 1960s and 70s during the Cultural Revolution, are once again freely practised. Millions of Chinese flock to museums, archaeological sites, the Forbidden City in Beijing, and Taoist and Buddhist temples and shrines, where they are surrounded by the traditional symbols of China, which are incorporated into the very fabric of the buildings. The same symbols are also found all over China in the patterns of the decorative arts and on textiles, in their ancient or more contemporary forms.

From the rise of their first imperial dynasties during the Bronze Age, the Chinese have used animal and plant symbols as talismans to ward off evil influences, disease and bad luck, and attract good luck, health and longevity. In the succeeding millennia they transmitted these symbols and their meanings to their neighbours, Korea, Japan, Mongolia and Vietnam. Some of the symbolic animals were previously unknown in their new homes, such as the tiger, which has never stalked the forests of Japan. Others have never existed, because they are creatures of the imagination and myth, such as the qilin and the phoenix. But once adopted, they have become part of the iconography of Asia, and in later times, of the vast East Asian world diaspora.

Western visitors to any area dominated by East Asian businesses will see animal and plant motifs wherever they turn. They might think of them purely as decorative patterns, but, in reality, they are the letters of an ancient East Asian alphabet of animal and plant symbols.

BIANFU (BAT)
happiness and longevity.
An ornate decorative symbol, it is painted
red – the colour of happiness.

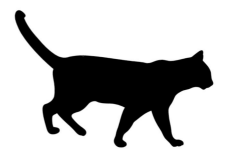

MAO (CAT)
omen of poverty.
Although unlucky, the cat is known
as the protector of silkworms.

GUAN (CRANE)
longevity.
The image of a crane is placed on
a coffin to bear the soul away.

QUAN (DOG)
protection and prosperity.
Fierce lion-dogs are found on guard outside
Chinese temples and palaces.

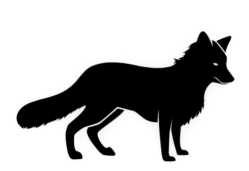

HULI (FOX)
transformation and trickery.
The fox is a shapeshifter that is able
to take on human form.

FENGHUANG (PHOENIX)
beauty and goodness.
The phoenix was used to decorate the
robes of the Chinese empress.

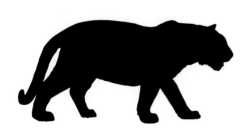

HU (TIGER)
courage and dignity.
The tiger was a talisman painted
on the shields of warriors.

QILIN (UNICORN)
gentleness and benevolence.
The unicorn was embroidered on the
robes of Chinese military officials.

LIANHUA (LOTUS)
purity and spiritual enlightenment.
Represents the seated 'lotus' posture
of the meditating Buddha.

TAO (PEACH)
marriage and immortality.
The peach tree of the gods was
thought to grant immortality.

SONG (PINE)
longevity and old age.
The sap of a thousand-year-old pine
was thought to turn into amber.

MEI (PLUM)
winter and longevity.
The sage Lao Tzu is said to have
been born under a plum tree.

SACRED TREES

Trees are rich in symbolism, both in cultures where they are plentiful and where they are a precious, scarce resource. They can represent both the positive aspects of nature and life – growth, fertility, renewal and spiritual awakening – and the negative – darkness, danger, the untamed wilderness and things that are forbidden. Trees can be symbols of the whole world with their roots deep in the underworld and their branches holding up the vault of heaven. In pagan lore, the forest can have two aspects: the grove dedicated to a deity where nature's bounty is celebrated, and the dark, dismal site of sacrifices and blood offerings.

We need look no further than the fir tree that people in many countries bring into their homes to celebrate Christmas Day. Although it may be synthetic and covered in garish tinsel, lights and baubles, the Christmas tree harks back to ancient Celtic, Norse, Slavic and Germanic Yuletide festivals when, on the shortest day of the year, branches of evergreen trees and bunches of mistletoe were brought into the home to symbolize the belief and hope that the old year had turned and that the new spring Sun would bring forth rebirth and renewal.

In Chinese lore, the promise of the peach tree is eternal youth and immortality, while pine and plum trees represent old age and longevity. In the foundational story cycle of Buddhism, Siddhartha Gautama attains enlightenment (*bodhi*) while seated in meditation for three days and nights under a fig tree, which bursts into bloom at the moment of his spiritual awakening. Trees can bring forth fruit that is physically and spiritually bountiful and nourishing, or which is forbidden, dangerous and even fatal. The fruit of the Tree of Life or Tree of Knowledge in the Garden of Eden, described in the scriptures of Judaism, Christianity and Islam, symbolizes the freedom that allows

human beings to choose between obedience or disobedience to God's law.

Trees can also represent the whole cosmos. In pagan Norse mythology, the world tree, Yggdrasil, is a giant ash that links the nine planes of existence, under whose boughs the gods, the Æsir, hold court. Similar all-encompassing world trees are known from cultures as diverse as ancient Iran, India and the pre-Columbian Americas.

Four representations of sacred trees, evidence of the cultural ubiquity of the tree as an occult symbol.

BODHI TREE, BUDDHIST

YGGDRASIL, NORSE

TREE OF LIFE, ASSYRIAN

TREE OF LIFE, CHRISTIAN

THE WHEEL
OF THE SEASONS

The adherents of various Neo-Pagan, Neo-Druidic, Rodnovery and Wicca traditions have created liturgical calendars, known as the 'Wheels of the Seasons' or 'Wheels of the Year', which subdivide the year according to the festivals of the ancient pagan Celts, Germans and Slavs. The eight spokes of the wheel mark the solstices and equinoxes and four other festivals celebrated in pre-Christian Europe.

There is little evidence to suggest that the ancient European Celts, Germans or Slavs observed a liturgical calendar as complex as the Wheel of the Seasons. The marking of the equinoxes and solstices would have been of interest to ritual specialists but not to agriculturalists, who could divine the timing of spring planting, calving and lambing from the observation of natural phenomena. The creation of the wheel is evidence of an ongoing transformation of Neo-Paganism, Neo-Druidism, Rodnovery and Wicca from a set of private magical practices into the public rituals of broader communities of believers.

The symbols on the wheel opposite correspond to the yearly festivals of the Celts, with the addition of a further four quarter- and cross-quarter-day festivals.

YULE
Yule marks the shortest day of the year, the winter solstice. The return of the Sun on the following dawn symbolized the turning of the year and presaged the return of life.

IMBOLC
Imbolc falls on the first of February and marks the beginning of spring. A time of purification, it was dedicated to the Celtic goddess Brigid.

OSTARA
Ostara marks the vernal equinox, when days and nights are once more equal in length, a presage of the warm, fruitful days to come.

BELTANE
Beltane, May Day, is traditionally the first day of summer in the Celtic year. It is a time when fertility is at its most potent.

LITHA
LItha marks the summer solstice and announces the turn of the year.

LAMMAS
Lammas, or August Eve, is a specifically Wiccan festival that marks the beginning of the harvest season with the symbolic eating of a bread effigy of the Celtic god Lugh.

MABON
Mabon marks the autumn equinox, when days and nights are again equal, but the year is waning. It is a festival of thanksgiving for the bounty of the Earth.

SAMHAIN
Samhain, or Halloween, celebrates the lives of ancestors, family members and loved ones who have died.

OGHAM TREE ALPHABET

The Celts occupied Europe during the Bronze and Iron ages, until they were displaced by successive waves of invaders. Their religion was a form of shamanism known as Druidism, whose beliefs centred around the regenerative powers of nature and tree lore. The Druids did not build wood or stone shrines but chose to perform their rituals in sacred groves. As the Celts in the British Isles faced mounting pressure from conquest and persecution, they preserved their traditional lore and esoteric knowledge by creating a sacred alphabet of trees, known as ogham. They carved ogham inscriptions on standing stones and on the wooden staves that they used for divination.

The Celts dominated the British Isles until the Roman conquest in the first century CE. Although the Romans did not replace the Celts, they suppressed Druidism, which they feared as a focus of resistance against their rule. After the Romans left Britain, the Celts were displaced by successive waves of invaders, beginning with the Anglo-Saxons and Vikings, and culminating with the Normans in the eleventh century. Though the Celts were gradually pushed to the fringes of the British mainland – Wales, Cornwall and Scotland – they remained dominant in Ireland for several more centuries; but, even here, Druidism faced persecution after the conversion of the island to Christianity in the fifth century.

The Celts created the ogham tree alphabet to preserve their traditions and esoteric lore. The largest body of ogham inscriptions in Ireland and Wales dates back to the fourth and sixth centuries. Although knowledge of ogham was never lost, it fell out of use until the revival of Druidism in Britain in the nineteenth century.

We know from Roman and Christian accounts of Druidic ceremonies that tree lore played a central role in Celtic religion. Pliny the Elder (c. 23–79 CE) describes how Druids cut mistletoe from sacred oak trees because they believed it imparted fertility. As well as the oak, the Druids held the other native trees and plants of the British Isles to be sacred and imbued with magical powers.

The seven symbols opposite represent both trees and letters of the ogham alphabet that were carved into staves for divination. The captions give the English name of each tree, its ogham name, the corresponding letter of the alphabet, day of the week and significance.

BIRCH

beith, B, Sunday, new beginnings.
The birch is a symbol of rebirth
and purification.

WILLOW

saille, S, Monday, intuition.
A willow symbol offers protection
from double-dealing.

HOLLY

tinne, T, Tuesday, protection and family.
Sacred to Taranis, the Celtic god
of lightning.

HAZEL

coll, C, Wednesday, wisdom and justice.
This symbol will assist in financial
and official dealings.

OAK

duir, D, Thursday, strength and power.
The king of the year from the winter
to the summer solstice.

APPLE

quert, Q, Friday, fertility and immortality
The apple was the symbol of love,
sex and fertility.

ALDER

fearn, F, Saturday, foundation and security.
The tree chosen for bridges and houses
built over water.

NATIVE AMERICAN MEDICINE WHEEL

For Native Americans, a medicine wheel can be both a metaphorical representation of sacred cosmological concepts and their embodiment in physical stone monuments that are used for religious rituals. Among the nomadic Plains Indian peoples, they could either be simple, temporary arrangements of small stones or large, permanent ceremonial structures aligned with the cardinal directions or with astronomical phenomena (the rising or setting points of the Sun, Moon and stars), rather like the megalithic monuments of Europe. The medicine wheel is divided into an outer wheel of four 'winds' and an inner wheel of twelve animal symbols.

The New World medicine wheel owes its name to its circular shape, with an outer rim and spokes radiating from a central hub, which is reminiscent of the shape of a Western astronomical chart or traditional depictions of the Chinese zodiac. It can vary from a few metres to 25 metres (27 yards) in diameter. Although the medicine wheel shares features with Old World systems of natal cosmological divination, in its conception and uses it is completely unique. As a metaphorical entity, the medicine wheel represents the never-ending cycles of nature and the 'sacred hoop' that binds the generations into one harmonious community.

As a physical monument, it served as a sacred space for the performance of ritual dances and other ceremonies, and as a calendar marking the solstices and the rising and setting of astronomical bodies; this served both ritual and practical uses, such as measuring time and marking the passage of the seasons.

There is no one standard form of the medicine wheel, and the one presented here is a synthesis of the many Native American traditions that have been passed down to the present day. On the outer wheel, the animals symbolic of the four winds are aligned to the cardinal directions and correspond to the seasons: East/Spring is represented by the eagle; South/Summer by the buffalo; West/Autumn by the bear; and North/Winter by the wolf. The inner wheel is occupied by twelve totemic animals, divided into groups of three (known as 'trines'), which function much like the star signs of Western astrology or the year animals of the Chinese zodiac, in that they indicate an individual's personal totem. A person's character can be determined by interpreting the relationship between a personal totem and its ruling wind.

The four outer animals or 'winds' indicate the cardinal points and seasons, and the twelve inner animals are personal totems.

FOUR WINDS & TWELVE TOTEMS

The four winds rule over four trines corresponding to the twelve months of spring, summer, autumn and winter. The relationship between wind, seasonality and the natural world can be seen in the selection of the four ruling and twelve totemic animals. For example, the butterfly and snake symbolize different aspect of transformation; the rabbit, fertility; and the raven, the positive and negative aspects of magic.

THE FOUR RULING ANIMALS

EAST, EAGLE, SPRING

Eagle is associated with new beginnings and approaches to life.

SOUTH, BUFFALO, SUMMER

Buffalo is associated with strength, generosity, hard work and perseverance.

WEST, BEAR, AUTUMN

Bear is associated with independence, self-sufficiency and careful planning.

NORTH, WOLF, WINTER

Wolf is associated with withdrawal, rest, recuperation and regeneration.

THE TWELVE TOTEMIC ANIMALS

East

HAWK
Ambition

BEAVER
Perseverance

DEER
Empathy

South

BUTTERFLY
Metamorphosis

SALMON
Permanence

RABBIT
Adaptability

West

RAVEN
Creation

FROG
Fertility

TURTLE
Patience

North

SNOW GOOSE
Dreams

OWL
Protection

SNAKE
Transformation

AUSTRALIAN ABORIGINAL DREAMING

Although the term 'dreaming' is a creation of European anthropologists, it is widely used in popular culture to define the cosmological concepts of the Australian Aboriginal peoples that fuse mythology, supernatural beings, totemic ancestors, custom, ritual, history and notions of belonging and identity with the physical geography of the vast Australian continent. In essence, a dreaming functions as a historical record and as a map of the physical world that identifies the landmarks, flora and fauna of a specific region. Other English terms that have been suggested to express this multifaceted cosmology include 'everywhen', 'world dawn' and 'ancestral present'.

Humans colonized the Australian continent between 50,000 and 60,000 years ago. Until the arrival of the first Europeans in the seventeenth century and their permanent colonization of the continent in the eighteenth, the Australian Aboriginal peoples developed in complete isolation from the rest of the world, creating a unique world view of such richness and complexity that it cannot be captured fully by the vague, nebulous terms 'dreaming' and 'dreamtime', used by European writers.

Among these English attempts to render the Aboriginal world view, 'everywhen' conveys notions of space and time in ways more reminiscent of advanced theoretical physics than mythology or history. A dreaming is a timeless act of creation that is repeated as one travels across the land, following and signing the 'dreaming tracks', or songlines, initially travelled and sung by supernatural entities as they brought the world into existence. Songlines explain the origins of the people, their connection to the land and its sacred sites, and how they became associated with a particular animal or plant totem, from which they trace their origins.

Although called 'divination' stones, the symbols overleaf cannot be used to foretell the future in the everywhen, in which past, present and future all exist at once and when and where cannot be distinguished. Rather than predict a future course of events, the stones reveal the inner intuitions that allow a person to shape them. The stones pair supernatural beings, totemic ancestors and natural phenomena that represent two aspects of a single principle; these are characterized as 'sunny' or 'shady', but without the Western connotations of good and bad that these terms might imply. A final stone is left blank for the All-Father, the formless creator god.

The Earth Sisters encounter the Rainbow Snake that will devour them.

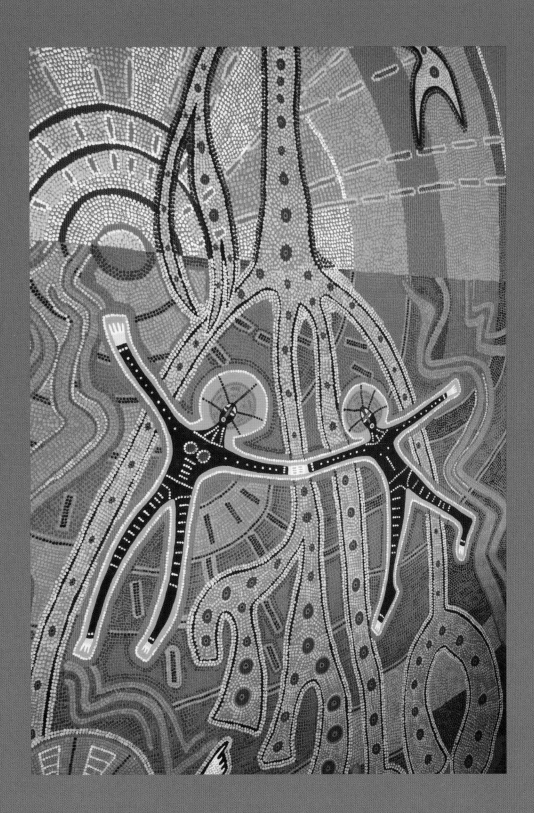

DIVINATION STONES

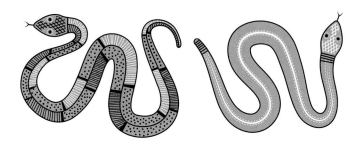

THE RAINBOW SNAKE AND THE BLACK-HEADED PYTHON

The Rainbow Snake is associated with water and is said to have created waterholes.
It becomes the Black-Headed Python when saved from the fire by the Storm Bird
that scorched its head.

THE HARE-WALLABY AND THE LIZARD WOMAN

The Hare-Wallaby and the Lizard Woman represent different aspects of human love;
the former, the innocent love of childhood; the latter, the love that brings sacrifice.

THE DINGO AND THE BLACK DOG

The Dingo is said to have brought law and custom to the Aboriginal peoples, while his pair, the Black Dog, symbolizes actions that fall outside law and custom.

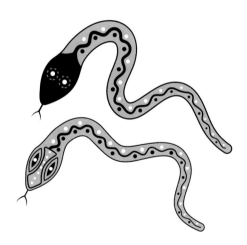

THE CARPET SNAKE AND THE POISONOUS SNAKE

Both the Carpet Snake and the Poisonous Snake are associated with the creation of the world's largest free-standing rock, Uluru. Both represent different types of altruism.

THE BLACK-THROATED BUTCHERBIRD
AND THE STORM BIRD

The Butcherbird protected the All-Father's secret knowledge from the
Rainbow Snake, while the Storm Bird saved him from the flames into
which he had been cast.

THE LIGHTNING BROTHERS
AND THE EARTH SISTERS

The Lightning Brothers are said to fight over one of their wives, causing storm
and rain, while the Earth Sisters were devoured by the rainbow snake who
henceforth spoke in their voices.

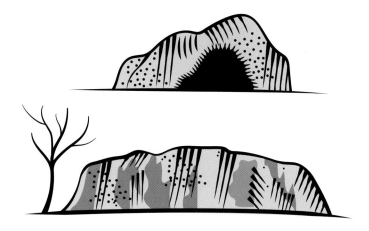

THE SACRED ROCK AND THE CAVE

The Sacred Rock represents the higher realms of the spirit and the Sky Heroes,
while the cave is associated with the womb of the Earth Mother, and the realms
of the subconscious and dreams.

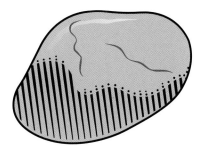

THE RAIN AND THE CLOUD

The rain and the cloud are two aspects of
the phenomenon of creation when male
and female are united.

THE ALL-FATHER

The stone signifying the creative force is left
blank because the All-Father is pure spirit
and has no physical form.

POLYNESIAN SYMBOLS

The one thousand islands of Polynesia account for a tiny fraction of the world's population, but they encompass a huge region of the Earth's surface, covering most of the central and south Pacific. The 'Polynesian Triangle' has Hawaii at its apex, and Aotearoa/New Zealand and Rapa Nui/Easter Island at its bottom left-hand and right-hand corners. Although separated by many thousands of miles of ocean, these far-flung island communities retain many social, cultural, linguistic and religious similarities, which are reflected in a shared iconography used to create jewelry, stone and wooden carvings, textile patterns and tattoo designs.

Beginning some 4,000 years ago, the ancestors of the inhabitants of Polynesia left their home on the island of Taiwan and embarked on successive waves of migration that lasted for the next four millennia. Instead of settling on the larger islands and landmasses they encountered, they pushed onwards to discover the myriad archipelagos of the Pacific. Ultimately, they did settle on the large islands of New Zealand/Aotearoa and are thought to have reached the western coasts of South America, though this reconnection with their distant Asian cousins, who had reached the Americas at least 15,000 years earlier, did not result in any lasting cultural exchanges.

These nomads of the ocean, whose love of travel led them to colonize islands as far from one another as Rapa Nui, Aotearoa, Hawaii and Tahiti, in the Polynesian Triangle, travelled in small sailing boats equipped with outriggers for speed and stability, without the benefit of the navigational aids and large ships of later European explorers. The Polynesians must have had an implicit faith in their gods and in their own skills as mariners, which would allow them to reach new landmasses, where they could settle or find fresh water and provisions.

Experts in the lore of oceanic winds and currents and in star navigation, the Polynesians depended on sea creatures such as the turtle, stingray and shark, which later became stylized motifs that they reproduced in wood and stone carvings, in textiles and on their own bodies in the form of tattoos, serving both as protective talismans and markers of social status. Alongside these are found terrestrial symbols associated with community and plant life, as well as symbols of the ocean that they thought of as their original home and the world beyond to which they returned after death.

MANAIA (MYTHICAL CREATURE)

spiritual messenger and guardian.
Head of a bird, tail of a fish, body of a man.

HAMMERHEAD SHARK

strength and fighting spirit.
The Maori believe sharks to be
protective spirits.

WHALE TAIL

protection of those at sea.
Whales are sacred protectors
of the Maori.

FERN FROND

life, growth, peace.
The young frond of the silver fern
common in New Zealand.

FISHHOOK

strength, determination, health.
The fishhook represents the bounty
of the sea and prosperity.

EMERGING PLANT LIFE

friendship and love.
Represents the eternal union
of two people or cultures.

FOETUS

good luck and fertility.
A representation of the unborn
foetus and the First Man.

STINGRAY

protection, agility, speed.
The stingray can hide from sharks
under the sand.

TURTLE

health, fertility, longevity.
The sea turtle symbolizes ocean travel
and navigation.

LIZARD

good or bad luck, omens.
Gods and spirits appear in the
form of lizards.

ENATA (HUMAN FIGURE)

humanity, relationships, defeated enemies.
Represents men, women and, sometimes,
the gods.

ENATA (REPEAT PATTERN)

sky, guardian ancestors.
Represents the ancestors protecting
their descendants.

OCEAN

death and the afterlife.
The place where people leave
for their last voyage.

SHARK TEETH

protection, guidance and strength.
Symbols of protection, ferocity
and adaptability.

SPEARHEAD

warrior spirit and danger from animals.
Symbolic of the warrior's courage
and of animal stings.

INDIAN SUBTLE ANATOMY

Indian and Western astrological traditions share the same origins in Greco-Babylonian astrology, brought to the Indian subcontinent by the Greeks in the fourth century BCE. In the fields of cosmology, religion, medicine and human anatomy, however, the Indian subjects of Alexander the Great and his successors did not adopt Greek ways, developing instead a unique corpus of observations, beliefs and practices that were codified in the scriptures and epics of Hinduism, the spiritual disciplines of Raja Yoga, and traditional Indian medicine, Ayurveda. Central to the practices of Yoga and Ayurveda are the concepts of the subtle anatomy, *prana* and the *chakras*.

In the Indian tradition, the eternal soul, or *atman*, is contained within three bodies: a mortal body of flesh, bone and blood, the *shtula sharira*; and two immortal bodies: the subtle, or astral, body, the *suksma sharira*; and the spiritual body, the *karana sharira*. By following the eight limbs of yoga, which include pranayama (breathing exercises) and hatha yoga (yoga of the posture), practitioners can train their mortal and immortal bodies to achieve *moksha* – liberation from the cycle of birth, death and rebirth – and attain *samadhi*, union with the transcendent Godhead known as Brahman. The suksma sharira is said to consist of the seven energy centres, the *chakras*, which are linked together by a central channel known as the *sushumna nadi*, through which flows the life force, *prana*, which is believed to animate the body and nourish the atman. The central nadi is also the conduit for the spiritual energy known as *kundalini* that is released during tantric practices. Two nadis intertwined around the sushumna, the *ida* and *pingala*, carry prana from the nostrils and distribute it throughout the mortal shtula sharira.

The chakras (literally 'wheels') are spaced along the sushumna nadi at key points where it connects to the network of lesser nadis that carry prana to the vital organs and limbs. Each chakra is attuned to a particular colour, pattern, element and *mantra* (sound). During practices such as pranayama, hatha yoga, meditation, visualization and chanting, prana is directed to the chakras. The lower chakras connect to the physical plane of existence, while the upper chakras are staging posts to higher states of consciousness, culminating in the highest chakra, *sahasrara* – the human connection with Brahman – which is simultaneously inside and outside the suksma sharira.

The subtle body, the suksma sharira, consisting of nadis and chakras, is shown superimposed on the mortal body of flesh and bone, the shtula sharira.

MULADHARA CHAKRA
ROOT

Colour: red; element: earth; mantra: *lam*;
petals: four

Located at the base of the spine, muladhara is our connection with the Earth. It rules the physical body and is the point of origin of kundalini spiritual energy. The four red petals are inscribed with the four *vritti* (modifiers of the mind) written in gold characters.

SWADHISHTANA CHAKRA
PELVIS

Colour: orange; element: water; mantra: *vam*;
petals: six

Located at the sexual organs, Swadhishtana controls sensuality and creativity. It is connected to the circulation of bodily fluids, including blood, urine and the sexual fluids. The six-petalled lotus contains a white crescent Moon and is associated with Varuna. Above the mantra is the *bindu* (dot) of Lord Vishnu.

MANIPURA CHAKRA
SOLAR PLEXUS

Colour: yellow; element: fire; mantra: *ram*;
petals: ten

Located in the solar plexus, manipura is the seat of our emotional being. It governs the body's glandular and nervous systems. The downward pointing triangle in the yellow circle is symbolic of the element fire. Often the petals are depicted in blue to be reminiscent of dark clouds in the sky.

ANAHATA CHAKRA
HEART

Colour: green; element: air; mantra: *yam*;
petals: twelve

Located at the heart, anahata is the chakra of love that governs relationships and attraction. It is an intermediary between the earthly and spiritual chakras. The two intersecting triangles known in the West as the Star of David is called the *shatkona* in Hinduism. It represents the god Siva and goddess Shakti.

VISHUDDHA CHAKRA
THROAT

Colour: blue; element: sound; mantra: *ham*;
petals: sixteen

Located at the throat, vishuddha governs communication and judgment. It rules all the anatomical structures around the throat including the vocal cords and thyroid gland. Surrounded by the sixteen petals is a downward-facing triangle within which sits a full Moon. The bindu above the mantra represents the god Sadashiva.

AJNA CHAKRA
THIRD EYE

Colour: indigo; element: light; mantra: *om*;
petals: two

Located in the middle of the forehead, ajna is the seat of intuition, inspiration, clairvoyance and wisdom. It is associated with the pituitary and pineal glands. The two petals of the Ajna Chakra represent the two nadi, *ida* and *pingala*; the petal on the left represents Siva, while the petal on the right represents Shakti.

SAHASRARA CHAKRA CROWN

Colour: white; element: thought; petals: infinite

Located just above the crown of the head, sahasrara is the chakra of divine purpose and connection to God. It is also associated with the pituitary and pineal glands. Said to be composed of an infinite number of petals that are simultaneously of all colours and colourless, it represents a transcendent union with godhead.

VODOU VÈVÈ

Between the sixteenth and nineteenth centuries, millions of African slaves were forcefully transported to the New World, initially to supplement and ultimately to replace the Native Caribbean workforce, decimated by war, mistreatment and European diseases. They brought with them their gods, myths and magical rituals, which over time they combined with figures from Native Caribbean and Catholic belief to create a syncretic religion, known to the people of Haiti as 'Serving the Spirits', and more popularly in the West as 'Voodoo', which is more properly spelt Vodou.

The origins of Haitian Vodou can be traced to the religions and magical practices of various African peoples, including the Yoruba of Nigeria, the Fon of Benin and the Kongo of Zaire (now Democratic Republic of the Congo). Transported to the West Indies to work in sugarcane plantations, they were forbidden to speak their own languages and practise their religions, and were forcefully converted to Christianity, in an attempt to subjugate them and prevent them from uniting and turning on their white oppressors.

Despite all these repressive measures, the slaves on the Spanish island of Hispaniola (present-day Haiti and the Dominican Republic) rebelled and won a hard-fought war of independence, creating the first Afro-Caribbean republic in the New World in 1804. Terrified that this might lead to further rebellions, slave owners did their best to demonize the Haitian Republic and its folk religion, Vodou, with sensational accounts of demonic possession, sorcery and zombies – stereotypes that have stuck, largely thanks to the fevered imaginings of Hollywood.

The creator god of the Vodou pantheon, Bondyé (from the French *Bon Dieu*), does not involve himself in human affairs. The links between the human and divine realms are mediated by the *loa* or *lwa*, supernatural entities thought to have their origins in the *vodun*, or tutelary spirits, of West Africa. Several loa are closely associated with Yoruba *orisha* (guiding spirits) and others with Catholic saints. During Vodou rituals, stylized diagrams called *vèvè*, symbolizing the different loa to be invoked, are drawn on the ground in flour, crushed eggshells or cornmeal. They act as channels for the loa to manifest themselves to receive the offerings and prayers of the worshippers. Like the orisha, the loa can 'ride' – that is, take possession of – their devotees, priests or priestesses, in order to perform the songs, dances and actions associated with them.

PAPA LEGBA
god of the crossroads,
the link between the human
and divine realms. His vèvè
symbolizes the crossroads
and an old man's crutch.

AGWÉ
god of the sea, wind and
thunder, associated with
St Ulrique. His vèvè is a
sailboat and his colours
blue and white.

DAMBALLAH
good serpent of the sky, god
of rain, streams and rivers.
His vèvè includes two snakes
reminiscent of the caduceus,
symbol of medicine and
alchemy.

ERZULIE
goddess of beauty who
represents the feminine
principle. Her vèvè
resembles the pierced
Catholic Sacred Heart of the
suffering Virgin Mary.

MAMAN BRIGITTE
goddess of life, death
and graveyards, who is
associated with St Brigid.
Her vèvè incorporates
graveyard motifs of
Christian crosses.

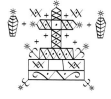

BARON SAMEDI
one of the Ghede, the loa
of the dead, who controls
sorcery and necromancy.
His vèvè is a stylized grave
with coffins.

BARON CIMETIÈRE
another of the Ghede, the
loa of the dead, who is the
guardian of graveyards. His
vèvè is a grave topped with
a human face.

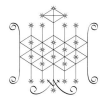
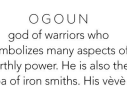

OGOUN
god of warriors who
symbolizes many aspects of
earthly power. He is also the
loa of iron smiths. His vèvè
resembles an iron grille with
palm-tree finials.

MEXICA GODS

The Aztecs, or to give them their proper name, the Mexica, used the fifty-two-year short count of the ritual Tzolk'in-Haab' ritual calendar (see page 30), but unlike their southern neighbours, the Maya, they did not have a fully functional script in which to write their language, Nahuatl. They produced books, known to us as 'codices', but rather than texts that could be read, these were illustrated aides-mémoire used to supplement knowledge that was preserved in oral traditions and re-enacted in public festivals. The Mexica worshipped a large pantheon of divinities, easily recognizable by their attributes, who governed every aspect of their lives, and whose survival depended on blood sacrifice.

The Mexica dominated central Mexico between about 1300 and the Spanish capture of their capital city, Tenochtitlán, in 1521. They believed that all aspects of life and nature were under the tutelage of specific gods and goddesses. Mexica cosmology held that the senior gods had created four preceding ages, or 'Suns', each of which had ended in cataclysmic destruction. They lived in fear of the end of the fifth age of the Sun, which would coincide with the return of the god Quetzalcoatl, the feathered serpent, who was expected to arrive over the sea from the west. The last Mexica ruler, Moctezuma II, mistakenly identified the Spanish conquistador Hernán Cortés as the returning Quetzalcoatl, marginally hastening the end of the fifth Sun and ensuring the destruction of Mexica civilization.

Mexico is an area prone to natural disasters – earthquakes, volcanic eruptions, floods and droughts – which the Mexica saw as evidence of the fragility of the world and presages of impending doom. They developed a unique mutually dependent relationship with their gods, who could not survive without human intervention. In order to ensure the survival of the fifth Sun, they needed to keep the gods strong by offering them the *tonalli,* or life force, of sacrificial victims, who could be captured enemy warriors, slaves, or Mexica chosen for the special characteristics that made them suitable as the sacrificial victims for a particular deity. Death by sacrifice was believed to guarantee a good afterlife.

Although the representations of the gods were not glyphs in the conventional sense, they acted as signifiers of the gods and goddesses of the Mexica pantheon, who could be readily identified by their stances, attributes, emblems and colours.

HUITZILOPOCHTLI

god of war and the Sun, patron god of the
Mexica. Represented as a hummingbird
or adorned with hummingbird feathers,
Huitzilopochtli carries a serpent-shaped
atlatl (spear thrower) and a mirror. As the
patron deity of the Mexica, he was one
of the two gods enshrined in the Templo
Mayor in Tenochtitlán.

TLALOC

god of rain, fertility and water, second in
importance to Huitzilopochtli. The second
deity enshrined in the Templo Mayor, Tlaloc
has large eyes and the fangs of a jaguar –
an animal sacrificed to the god alongside
children who were offered to ensure the
coming of the rains.

TEZCATLIPOCA

god of hurricanes, divination and sorcery. Tezcatlipoca
translates as smoking mirror. He is associated with obsidian,
a kind of volcanic glass used to make Mexica weapons and
polished to create mirrors that were used in divination rituals.
His face is covered with yellow and black stripes.

QUETZALCOATL

god of wind, air and learning. Quetzalcoatl,
in the guise of the feathered serpent, is
an enduring divinity in the Mesoamerican
pantheon that long predates Mexica
domination of the region. A temple to the
god is one of the main structures in the
central Mexican site of Teotihuacán,
built *c.* 150–200 CE.

CHALCHIUHTLICUE

goddess of waters, streams and storms.
Chalchiuhtlicue, 'She of the Jade Skirt', is
often depicted with water flowing from
underneath her skirt as a symbol of the
fertility born of the waters. She is also the
patroness of midwives and childbirth.

MICTLANTECUHTLI

god of the dead and the underworld. As befits the Lord
of the Underworld, Mictlantecuhtli is represented as a
skeleton with a necklace of human eyeballs. He is related to
the representations of the dead during the contemporary
Mexican Day of the Dead festival.

TLAZOLTEOTL

goddess of filth, vice and purification.
Tlazolteotl is the goddess of filth and sin,
and of purification and the forgiveness of
sin. She was also associated with venereal
diseases, with which she afflicted those
engaging in sinful or forbidden love.

XIPE TOTEC

god of the spring and renewal. Xipe Totec
flayed himself, shedding his skin like a
moulting snake or a maize seed before
it germinates to feed humanity. He is
represented wearing the flayed human
skin of one of his sacrificial victims.

TECCIZTECATL

god of the Moon. Tecciztecatl competed with another god
to become the Sun so that there were two suns in the sky.
The gods threw a rabbit at Tecciztecatl, dimming his light
and creating the rabbit pattern on the surface of the Moon.

SACRED WRITINGS

The advent of writing transformed the world in two very
different ways: first, it enabled humans to keep a faithful
record of their history and customs – something hitherto
entrusted to human memory that could be falsified or
forgotten; second, the belief that the act of writing the
name of something allowed people to conjure or control
it led them to create a written corpus of magico-religious
rituals, whose faithful performance, they believed,
gave them the ability to change the world and
the course of future events.

Humans devised writing for two very different purposes: the first was practical, to facilitate taxation and civil administration and create permanent records of commercial contracts and property ownership; the second was to preserve and transmit the sacred traditions and ritual practices that regulated the relationships between humanity and the gods. Writing was a solution to the fallibility of human memory, while it also provided a new means to falsify it. At the same time, it became the principal medium used to transform and control the world through magic and ritual.

We cannot conceive of a time when writing did not exist, when all knowledge had to be stored inside people's heads in the form of oral traditions, which could be purposefully or accidentally misremembered, or forgotten altogether. The first uses of pictograms were for inventories or bills of sale; for example, to record how many cattle, sheep or bushels of grain were to be delivered to the palace or temple as tithe or tax. To the illiterate drover or farmer who paid his taxes in kind, the sight of a scribe writing abstract symbols that mysteriously conveyed what should be delivered to an official receiving the animals and grain many miles away, must have seemed like magic – or monstrous sorcery – because it prevented him from cheating the tax officials.

The written word changed the way the world worked, and it took a very small mental jump to believe that the name of something written down was equivalent to the thing itself. From this association, emerged the many traditions of text-based ceremonial magic that created a corpus of incantations, spells, curses and talismans.

Over the millennia, pictograms became ever more abstract, and the signs that had once stood for a whole word could be used to write syllables or single letters. As writing matured, so did the grammar and spelling of the languages it conveyed, increasing the nuances of what could be expressed, such as the tenses of verbs, and the gender and number of nouns, and adjectives.

Egyptian pharaohs and Assyrian kings had their achievements and victories memorialized in stone inscriptions on temple and palace walls, but are we sure they were telling the truth? We only have their written word for it. Priests and occultists compiled permanent records of holy texts and detailed descriptions of ritual, preserving their beliefs and practices for millennia – powerful magic indeed.

Sixth-century BCE inscription from Ishtar Gate, the eighth gate to the inner city of Babylon, Iraq.

CUNEIFORM

The Sumerians devised the first written signs in the Near East, known to us as cuneiform, which remained in continuous use for over three millennia, making it one of humanity's longest-lived writing systems. During this vast span of time, cuneiform was adapted to write several different languages and employed for a wide variety of uses, including commercial and legal documents, works of literature and poetry, historical chronicles, royal inscriptions and dedications, astrological treatises and books of divination, magical spells and hymns to the gods.

Sumer, in the southernmost part of Mesopotamia (roughly corresponding to modern Iraq), has long been regarded as the cradle of urban civilization. Cuneiform was created there around 3,500 years BCE and remained in use until the first centuries CE. It was used to write a succession of Near Eastern languages, including Sumerian, Akkadian, Hittite, Elamite, Babylonian, Assyrian and Persian. Additionally, it was the preferred script for diplomatic correspondence during the Bronze Age.

Cuneiform originated in simple pictographic signs impressed on clay tokens that were the Sumerian equivalent of bills of sale and inventories of goods, grain and livestock. Despite its rather mundane origins in accounting and commerce, by the turn of the third millennium BCE cuneiform had evolved into the region's first abstract script. To the largely illiterate populations of Mesopotamia, it must have appeared supernatural. When they saw officials, priests and scribes write abstract signs for the words 'ox' or 'sheep', they may have credited them with the magical power of controlling animals, or even with the godlike attribute of calling them into being. In ceremonial magic, the writing of a supernatural being's true name has long been equated with the ability to conjure and control them. Hence, the invention of cuneiform quickly prompted the development of written prayers, incantations, spells and curses.

Once perfected, cuneiform was quickly co-opted for a huge range of profane and sacred uses. The dedicatory stone tablet shown opposite depicts a supplicant Babylonian king being led into the presence of the sun god, Shamash, whose blazing sun disc rests on an altar in front of his throne, and above whose head are three divine symbols: the lunar disc of the moon god Sin, his own solar disc and the eight-pointed star of Ishtar, the goddess of the planet Venus.

A Babylonian king is led in front of the sun god, with cuneiform inscriptions describing the scene, its participants and its royal dedication.

THE CUNEIFORM SCRIPT

The name 'cuneiform' is derived from the Latin word *cuneus*, meaning 'wedge', because the ideograms are constructed from wedge-shaped or nail-shaped marks. To write cuneiform, a stylus with a suitably shaped tip was pressed into the surface of an unbaked clay tablet. If what was written was ephemeral, the tablet could be moistened and the stylus marks erased. But if the text was to be preserved, the tablet was baked to create an indestructible record. At least half a million clay tablets have been discovered so far, and more are unearthed from Near Eastern sites every year. Tablets were also baked inadvertently when a building was destroyed in an accidental fire or when a city was sacked and burned.

In their first iteration, Sumerian pictograms were written with a rounded stylus and did not have the script's characteristic wedge-shaped appearance. The signs shown in the first column opposite are pictograms, that is, recognizable depictions of the object denoted. Even when the sign stands for a more abstract concept, such as those for 'destiny' and 'ruler', the visual association is clear: 'destiny' is based on the pictogram for a bird in flight, and 'ruler' is the pictogram for a man wearing a headdress or crown.

As the script evolved, the signs were rotated ninety degrees (column two). In column three, the signs have become recognizably cuneiform, incised with a wedge-shaped stylus. Although they retain the same basic form, they have become more abstract and less obvious to read. The last two columns demonstrate how the signs were further abstracted into true ideograms that only a trained scribe could interpret.

The script's structure also became more abstract. While, in the original pictographic script, the pictogram for 'ox' would also signify the sound of the word *ox*, in later cuneiform the signs could represent syllables or single letters, so that several signs could be joined together to create words and names unconnected with the original meanings of the component signs. The inscription given below reads 'Assurbanipal, King of Assyria' in the much older Sumerian cuneiform (above) and in Assyrian cuneiform (below). Assurbanipal ruled the Assyrian empire in the seventh century BCE, 1,600 years after the invention of cuneiform in ancient Sumer.

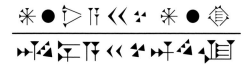

	Sumerian Vertical	**Sumerian** Rotated	**Babylonian** Early	**Babylonian** Late	**Assyrian**
Star					
Ruler					
Power					
Ox					
Destiny					
Dwelling					

MESOPOTAMIAN CIVILIZATION

The rival city-states of Sumer each had their own patron deity. The most important building in the centre of the city was the temple built on top of a stepped pyramid known as a 'ziggurat', which was both the cult centre of the city and the residence of the city's patron god or goddess. We think of a city as built for the benefit of its citizens, but the Sumerians believed that cities were the homes of the gods, whom all citizens, from the king and high priest down to the lowliest artisan and farmer, worshipped and served.

The notion that the sole purpose of the city was the service and glorification of its patron deity was transmitted to the Babylonians. When they dominated Mesopotamia and beautified their city, they did so in the name of their patron god Marduk, whose image resided in the holy of holies on top of the city's ziggurat. The god's apartments were adorned with golden furniture and his statue was cared for by priests and priestesses as if it were a living being that required to be dressed, fed and entertained. In a very real sense, everything that pertained to the city was sacred because it belonged to the god.

The Sumerian titles *lugal* and *ensi*, which are usually translated as 'king' and 'high priest', designated servants of the patron god or goddess, entrusted as the city's leading representatives and as the stewards of the city – a little like Renaissance popes who were heads of the Roman Church and temporal rulers of the Papal States, and who occasionally led their armies in the field of battle.

The four illustrations opposite show different ritual uses of cuneiform. The first is a temple dedication, known from its shape as a 'nail cone'. Interred in the foundations, it credits the royal builder who had honoured his city's patron deity. Although the king claims the credit, the form of words reflects

his status as the god's humble servant. The last three are astronomical and astrological documents used in divination – not as an individual horoscopic chart such as we might commission today, but for matters concerning the ruler as the representative of the city and the principal official of its god.

SUMERIAN TEMPLE
DEDICATION (NAIL CONE)
c. 2200–2100 BCE

BABYLONIAN
ASTROLOGICAL CHART
c. 3000 BCE

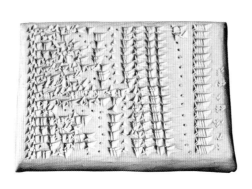

BABYLONIAN STAR LIST
c. 400–200 BCE

ASSYRIAN MAP OF
THE HEAVENS
c. 3400–3300 BCE

EGYPTIAN HIEROGLYPHS

Even after ancient Egypt lost its political independence, when it became part of a succession of larger Eurasian empires, beginning with the Assyrians, who were followed by the Persians, Macedonian Greeks and Romans, it displayed a conspicuous cultural continuity expressed in the iconography of its traditional artistic and architectural styles, its religion, its burial customs, and of its hieroglyphic script. Although it has been suggested that the Egyptians learned to write from the Sumerians, it is more likely that the two writing systems emerged independently during the fourth millennium BCE.

The hieroglyphic writing system was extremely complex, consisting of between 900 and 1,000 different symbols that could be used as logograms standing for a whole word, to represent single letter sounds and as determinatives, signs that were not meant to be voiced but were inserted to clarify the meanings of classes of words, such as personal names or the grammatical components of a sentence. This complexity meant that true literacy was the preserve of scribes or priests.

Like cuneiform, the Egyptian writing system developed simpler, more abstract forms known as hieratic and demotic for everyday purposes. The ancient pictographic hieroglyphic signs continued to be used for monumental inscriptions and for magical texts, such as the Book of the Dead, whose spells were incised or painted on the walls of tombs and on sarcophagi to help the deceased negotiate the many perils of the underworld and to achieve immortality in the afterlife. The notion that the written sign was imbued with magical power was common in Egypt, as evidenced by numerous protective talismans used by the living and by the placing of precious hieroglyphic amulets within the wrappings of Egyptian mummies. This practice meant

that grave robbers always desecrated the mummies of the tombs they looted, decapitating them and tearing off their protective bandages to obtain the valuable amulets.

The name of the deceased was always prominently displayed in Egyptian burials so that the gods would be in no doubt as to his identity. In the tomb of the Pharaoh Tutankhamun, the cartouches containing his name and regnal title are found reproduced on the doorway and walls, on his coffins and all the grave goods interred with him. Overleaf is a sample of hieroglyphs, giving their sacred meanings.

Tomb painting of an Egyptian couple relaxing at home. It depicts the deceased sitting next to his wife and playing chess or checkers.

EGYPTIAN HIEROGLYPHS

ANKH

Life and resurrection

SENEB

Health and wellbeing

BOAT

Transmigration and
celestial journey

WEDJA

Material prosperity

KHEFER

Creation and rebirth

NEFER

Goodness and beauty

DJED

Stability and strength

IB

Source of the life force

PILLOW

Protection at night
and in death

WADJET

Protection from evil

MENAT

Fertility and joy

NEKHBET

Purification and renewal

GOLD COLLAR

Detachment and
renunciation

LADDER

Transition to the afterlife

SHEN

Infinity and permanence

MINOAN PICTOGRAMS (PHAISTOS DISC)

The artefact known as the Phaistos Disc is one of the most enigmatic archaeological finds ever made on the island of Crete. The baked clay disc, which is 15 cm (6 in.) in diameter, is unlikely to impress museum visitors who expect ancient treasures to be made of solid gold studded with precious stones. Nevertheless, it is priceless in archaeological terms because of its uniqueness. Nothing similar has ever been found in the whole of the Eastern Mediterranean region. More puzzling still, since its discovery in 1908, the pictograms stamped onto the two sides of the disc remain undeciphered.

The Phaistos Disc is named for the place it was found, the Minoan palace complex of Phaistos on the Greek island of Crete. It was unearthed during excavations at the turn of the twentieth century, at the same time as Sir Arthur Evans was excavating the now much more famous Minoan palace complex of Knossos, made famous for its association with the legend of King Minos who imprisoned his monstrous bull-headed son, the Minotaur, in a labyrinth. The mysterious pictograms, stamped on both sides of the disc in a spiral pattern, immediately attracted the attention of archaeologists and scholars, who continue to speculate as to its function and origins, which range from a game board or religious text to the earliest example of movable type created by some unknown Cretan genius.

The Minoans used a syllabic script known as Linear A, whose code is also yet to be cracked, but its component signs are not those found on the disc. There are 241 pictograms on the disc, which are made up of an 'alphabet' of forty-five signs arranged in groups varying in length from two to six, separated by incised lines, suggesting that they might represent words.

It seems probable that the two sequences are text, because a game board would more likely consist of single squares. The location where the disc was unearthed also suggests that it was a precious, sacred artefact. The disc was interred in a dedicatory deposit underneath the ceremonial gateway of the Phaistos palace complex, along with the bones and ashes of sacrificial animals and a tablet written in Linear A. Deposits of precious, sacred objects indicated the importance of the building and provided it with magical protection.

Above – Knossos palace ruins, Crete, Greece.

Opposite – More than a century after its discovery on Crete, the disc is yet to be deciphered.

PHAISTOS DISC PICTOGRAMS

RUNNING
MAN

ARROW

PLANE

HOOF

PAPYRUS

CRESTED
HELMET

BOW

STORAGE
JAR

CAT

FLOWER

TATTOOED
FACE

SHIELD

COMB

RAM

LILY

CAPTIVE

CLUB

SLING

FLYING
BIRD

OX BACK

CHILD

MANACLE

MALLET

PIGEON

FLUTE WOMAN AXE BEEHIVE FISH GRATER

HELMET DAGGER BOAT BEE SIEVE HAND

LID HORN TREE HAND AXE HEAD-DRESS SET SQUARE

OX HIDE OLIVE TREE WATER

ANCIENT GREEK ALPHABET & NUMERALS

The ancient Greeks are credited with the invention of philosophy, mathematics and the scientific method, so the reader might wonder why their alphabet and numbers are included in a book of occult symbols, but their rationality and scepticism only represented one part of their world view. Highly superstitious and religious, they lived in fear of the gods and other supernatural entities and often resorted to magic, divination, astrology and oracles. The ancient Greeks believed in the magical power inherent in writing, and they also devised the occult science of numerology, the art of divination by numbers.

The Greeks were comparative latecomers to writing compared with the Sumerians and Egyptians. They obtained a ready-made alphabet from the Phoenicians, which they adapted to their linguistic needs. One of the great advantages that they derived from this cultural appropriation was that the Phoenician alphabet was made up of two dozen signs that were easy to memorize, read and write, making literacy much more attainable than in cultures with complex pictographic and ideographic writing systems. In ancient Greece, you did not have to be a scribe or ritual specialist to create magic formulae from the Greek alphabet, which used the same characters for letters and numerals.

The letters of the Greek alphabet are now associated with mathematics and the sciences, but in ancient times, there was less of a demarcation between the natural sciences that sought to understand the cosmos and the magical and ritual practices that sought to control it. An exemplar of this fusion of scientific and magical thinking was the sixth-century BCE mathematician and mystic, Pythagoras. We remember him today for his eponymous theorem about right-angled triangles, but he also devised a method of alphabetic and numerological divination that ascribed numbers to the letters in a person's name, which, when combined with their date of birth, was believed to reveal a person's character and destiny.

Greek remained the sacred language of Christianity long after Greece fell to the Muslim Ottoman Turks. The earliest-known copies of the New Testament were written in Greek. The Greek versions of the Gospels are considered to be among the most authoritative and were the basis for the translations of Christian scripture into Latin and are still used now for the translation and exegesis of the books of the New Testament.

Carved ancient Greek inscriptions used capital letters, while upper- and lower-case script were used for handwritten texts.

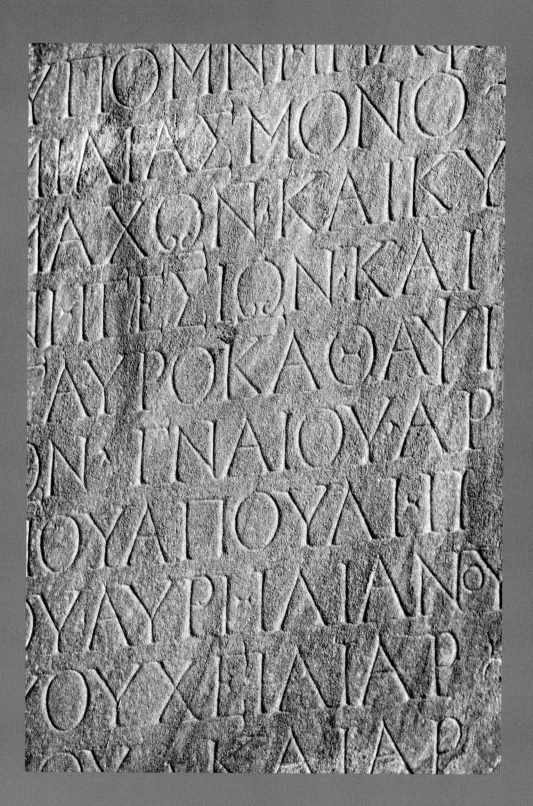

GREEK ALPHABET

Αα′	Ββ′	Γγ′	Δδ′	Εε′
ALPHA	BETA	GAMMA	DELTA	EPSILON

Ζζ′	Ηη′	Θ θ′	Ιι′	Κκ′
ZETA	ETA	THETA	IOTA	KAPPA

Λλ′	Μμ′	Νν′	Ξξ′	Οο′
LAMBDA	MU	NU	XI	OMICRON

Ππ′	Ρρ′	Σσ′	Ττ′	Υυ′
PI	RHO	SIGMA	TAU	UPSILON

Φφ′	Χχ′	Ψψ′	Ωω′
PHI	CHI	PSI	OMEGA

GREEK NUMERALS

α′	β′	γ′	δ′	ε′
1	2	3	4	5
ς′	ζ′	η′	θ′	ι′
6	7	8	9	10
κ′	λ′	μ′	ν′	ξ′
20	30	40	50	60
ο′	π′	ϟ′	ρ′	σ
70	80	90	100	200
τ′	υ′	φ′	χ′	ψ′
300	400	500	600	700
ω′	ϡ′			
800	900			

CELTIC SYMBOLS & KNOTS

The Celts consisted of a disparate group of pagan peoples, linked by cultural, linguistic and religious similarities, who lived from the Iberian Peninsula in the west to Asia Minor in the east – a vast geographical area matched by the vast span of time during which they dominated most of the European continent. Today, they are best remembered for the complex, interlaced designs, referred to as 'Celtic knots', which were pagan in origin but were repurposed for Christian use.

In the British context, Celtic culture is associated with the 'Celtic fringe' of Scotland, Ireland, Wales and Cornwall – the more isolated and easily defensible western regions of the British Isles, where the original Celtic Britons were driven to seek refuge from waves of Anglo-Saxon and Norse invaders, who came, first as raiders and then settlers, between the fifth and eleventh centuries CE.

The symbols associated with the Celts are extremely ancient, dating back to prehistoric times, and they occur over a huge geographical area. Celtic motifs, such as the 'triskelion' and 'triquetra', are also found in the artistic canons of ancient Greece and Rome and were later adopted by the Germanic peoples who migrated into the Roman Empire, displacing both its original Celtic inhabitants and their Roman overlords.

Although they were pagan in origin, Celtic symbols were adapted for Christian use, first in Ireland, which was Christianized in the fifth century CE, developing its own native Celtic Christian tradition, and later in Anglo-Saxon England, which was evangelized by missionaries sent by the Roman Church in the seventh century. Notable Christian Celtic symbols include the 'Celtic High Cross', with its trademark nimbus, or halo, around the intersection of the arms of the cross, and the 'St Brigid's Cross', which was appropriated by the Irish Church from the pagan cult of the Celtic goddess Brigid.

The interlaced lines of Celtic symbols, often referred to as 'Celtic knots', are based on rope and basket-weaving knots. They were used extensively to decorate early illuminated manuscripts of Christian scripture, on carved ornaments in churches, and on crosses and tombstones in the Celtic lands and in Europe more widely during the medieval period, as decorative elements of the high Gothic cathedral style.

Above – Illumination from the Book of Kells, *c. 800 CE.*

SAILOR'S KNOT

TRISKELION

TRIQUETRA

CELTIC CROSS

BOWEN KNOT

SOLOMON'S KNOT

ST BRIGID'S CROSS

TREE OF LIFE

LAUBURU CROSS

WEDDING KNOT

ANGLO-SAXON RUNES

The runic alphabet is a relic of the age of migrations that spans the whole of the first millennium CE, which reshaped the cultural and ethnic map of Europe. The first wave overran the Western Roman Empire, including the Roman provinces of Britannia, invaded by the Angles and Saxons from continental Frisia and Denmark in the fifth century; the second saw the Norse people raid the coasts of western Europe and establish the Danelaw in eastern England.

Runic alphabets first appeared around the year 150 CE and subsisted in western and central Europe until their Christianization in the eighth century and until the twelfth century in northern Europe. The script went through three major iterations and several minor ones. Elder Futhark runes lasted from 150 to 800 to be replaced by Younger Futhark runes, from 800 to 1100. The Anglo-Saxons created the longer 30-character Futhorc runic alphabet featured opposite, which they used from the fifth century until their defeat by the Normans in the eleventh century. As this was not a standardized alphabet, the translations given are speculative. Even once the whole of Europe had adopted Christianity and the Latin alphabet, runes continued to feature in anthologies of the Viking epic poems compiled in Iceland and Scandinavia from the thirteenth century onwards.

The first-century CE Roman historian Tacitus, in his book *Germania*, describes a possible use of runes for divination, though he doesn't use the term rune or describe the appearance of the symbols used by Germanic diviners. More securely attested is the use of runic magic in the eighth-, ninth- and tenth-century poems anthologized in the *Poetic Edda* (see page 102). In the 'Sigrdrífumál', the Valkyrie Sigrdrífa counsels

a hero about the magical use of runes. She tells him to carve the rune Tyr, also Teiwaz, associated with the Germanic Zeus, to ensure victory in battle. Other runes will protect him from witchcraft and his longboat from shipwreck.

Runic inscriptions have also been found on standing stones in burial fields all over the Norse and Germanic world. These inscriptions threaten anyone who dares desecrate the burials, rich in precious grave goods, armour and weaponry, with the most terrible punishments and slow, lingering painful deaths.

RUNES

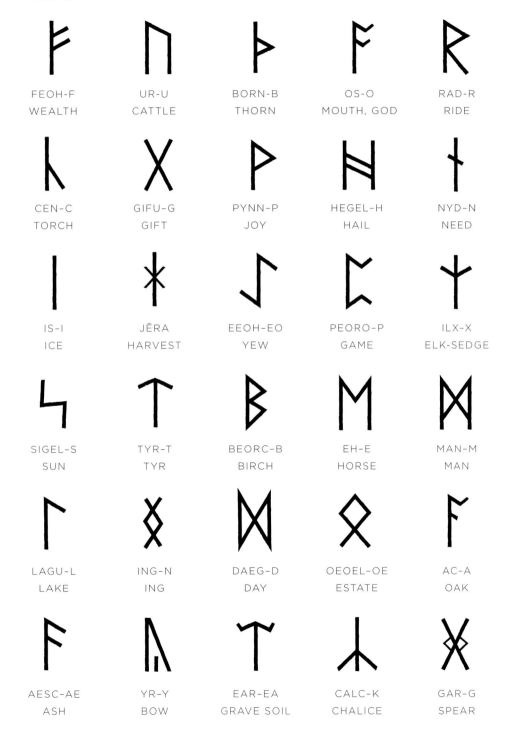

FEOH-F
WEALTH

UR-U
CATTLE

BORN-B
THORN

OS-O
MOUTH, GOD

RAD-R
RIDE

CEN-C
TORCH

GIFU-G
GIFT

PYNN-P
JOY

HEGEL-H
HAIL

NYD-N
NEED

IS-I
ICE

JĒRA
HARVEST

EEOH-EO
YEW

PEORO-P
GAME

ILX-X
ELK-SEDGE

SIGEL-S
SUN

TYR-T
TYR

BEORC-B
BIRCH

EH-E
HORSE

MAN-M
MAN

LAGU-L
LAKE

ING-N
ING

DAEG-D
DAY

OEOEL-OE
ESTATE

AC-A
OAK

AESC-AE
ASH

YR-Y
BOW

EAR-EA
GRAVE SOIL

CALC-K
CHALICE

GAR-G
SPEAR

ICELANDIC STAVES

Galdrastafur, Icelandic magical staves, are a type of magical sigil used in Iceland between the fourteenth and seventeenth centuries. Although they have been linked to earlier traditions of pagan Germanic and Norse runic magic, the association is tenuous because runes were replaced by the Latin alphabet when Iceland was converted to Christianity around the year 1000 CE. The true origins of galdrastafur are probably not to be found in Iceland's Viking past but in the fusion of Renaissance ceremonial magic with Christian symbolism.

Galdrastafur exist in the grey area where pictograms and ideograms overlap with visual symbols. The staves cannot be 'read' like ideograms that represent whole words, syllables or letters, but each has a voiced name that conveys a set meaning, which would have been known to the Icelandic population of the late medieval and early modern periods. What really fits them into the category of magical 'writings' is how they were used: they were written on trees, the doorposts of houses and rocks, as well as on portable items, such as wooden staffs, or on small pieces of wood or bark that could be hidden in shoes or clothing.

Galdrastafur are known from Icelandic grimoires (books of magic, see page 213) that date from the seventeenth century or later. Some of their constituent elements are derived from Christian symbolism, others from Renaissance occultism and some have been tenuously linked with Norse and Germanic runes that were used in Iceland until it was converted to Christianity around the year 1000 CE. The 400-year interval between Norse runes and galdrastafur most likely means that their associations are more imaginary than real.

There is one exception, however, Ægishjálmur, the Helm of Awe, which is mentioned in the *Poetic Edda*, a thirteenth-century anthology of much earlier epic poems, that recounts how the hero Sigurðr slays the dragon Fáfnir and obtains the Helm of Awe, which is not a helmet worn on the head but a kind of protective aura that allows him to defeat his enemies. The other staves reproduced opposite have much more modest aims as protective talismans and good luck charms. The two galdrastafur Gapaldur and Ginfaxi were to be inserted in one's shoes – under the heel of the right foot and under the toes of the left, to ensure that the wearer would win his wrestling bouts.

GINFAXI
Success in wrestling

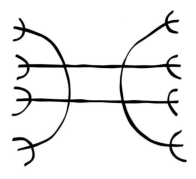

GAPALDUR
Success in wrestling

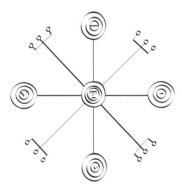

VELÖLSTAFUR
Good luck in fishing

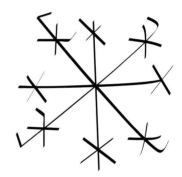

ÞJÓFASTAFUR
Protection against thieves

ÆGISHJÁLMUR
The Helm of Awe

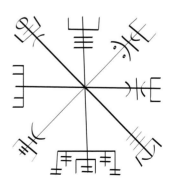

VEGVISIR
Protection in bad weather

ADINKRA

The Adinkra motifs that decorate the mass-produced fabrics of the Ashanti region of Ghana have their origins in designs intended for the exclusive use of the kings of Gyaman in neighbouring Ivory Coast. When the Ashanti Kingdom conquered Gyaman, its kings appropriated the manufacture and use of Adinkra fabrics. The motifs are not purely decorative but constitute an 'alphabet' of symbols that represent plants, animals and everyday objects, which stand for aphorisms relating to the royal family and daily life, sometimes in a humorous fashion, while also acting as protective talismans.

British readers will be familiar with the system of warrants that allows a business to print 'By royal appointment' on their products as a royal seal of approval. The Adinkra cloth motifs have the extra cachet of not only being worn by royalty but also of having been designed by royalty. The eighteenth-century ruler of the kingdom of Gyaman, Nana Kwadwo Agyemang Adinkra, designed the cloth motifs to which he also gave his name. When the conquering Ashanti forced the king and his heir to give them the secrets of the cloth's manufacture and design, they adopted them for their own royal family.

King Nana Kwadwo did not invent the Adinkra motifs themselves, which were already in use on pottery, ceremonial gold regalia and on the carved wooden stools that symbolize authority in this region of West Africa. He created Adinkra fabrics for his personal use at important state occasions, and they were also adopted by high-ranking members of his court. Initial designs were much more restrained than the brightly coloured fabrics that are characteristic of today's Adinkra.

Royal Gyaman Adinkra cloth was hand-printed with stamps made from calabash gourds in a monochrome ink made from tree roots and bark on plain red, dark brown or black fabric, depending on the ceremony and the wearer's role in it. An early example, acquired by a British visitor in the early nineteenth century, features sixteen squares of Adinkra symbols printed in black on a plain background that the king wore as a mourning cloth at funerals.

The sample motifs reproduced overleaf capture the mix of everyday observations and protective symbols of traditional Adinkra.

A display of modern, brightly coloured Ghanaian kente cloth stamped with Adinkra motifs.

ADINKRA

ABAN
Reserved for
the king

AKOMA NTOASO
Conjoined hearts

BI NNKA BI
Don't injure others

DAME DAME
Intelligence and
ingenuity

HYE WO NHYE
The arsonist won't be
burned

MUSUDEYIDIE
To ward off evil

NKONSONKONSON
Chains or manacles

GYE NYAME
For God alone

NKOTIMSEFUOPUA
The hairstyles
of court ladies

NSIREWA
Cowrie shells
(used as currency)

NSOROMA
Child of God

MASIE
Keeping confidences

NYAME DUA
Altar to Sky God

NYAME NWU NA MAWU
May Nyame die
before me

OHEN' TUO
The king's gun

SANKOFA
Learn from the past

NKYIMKIM
Twisted rope

SEPOW
To prevent a condemned
man from cursing
the king

CHINESE ORACLE BONE SCRIPT

The earliest form of Chinese divination dates back to the Shang dynasty, which ruled north-eastern China during the latter half of the second millennium BCE. The practice is known as 'oracle bone divination' from its use of animal bones and tortoise shells, on whose polished surfaces diviners carved or brushed questions in a script that is recognizably the precursor of the ideographic scripts that are still used in China, Japan and Korea today.

Unlike the more democratic divination method of the *I Ching* that the Chinese still use today, oracle bone divination was abandoned in the first millennium BCE. Its heyday was the second millennium BCE, but even then its use was limited to the highest echelons of Shang dynasty society – the ruler himself and members of the royal family. It fell out of favour, in part, because of the complexity of the oracular method and the cost of the materials required to perform it: the shoulder bones of full-grown oxen and the shells of land tortoises – the latter gifted to the king of Shang as tribute from vassal states. Although ancient China was a highly literate culture, during the Shang dynasty it is likely that only members of the royal court and its scribes and ritual specialists had the leisure time, or the need, to learn to read and write.

In order to perform an oracle, the bone or shell had to be prepared. After it was scraped clean of flesh and polished smooth, a series of regularly spaced rows of hollows or dips were drilled into the surface. Finally, it was anointed with blood and inscribed with the date of the ceremony. The oracle proper could now be performed. The topic of the oracle was carved onto the shell or bone, or less frequently written with brush and ink, using a distinctive oracle script.

Questions included personal matters affecting the ruler and his family, such as illness and death, as well as matters of state. One of the most common questions concerned the correct procedure to perform rituals to honour the ancestors. At this point, the diviner or the ruler himself inserted a source of heat, such as a piece of heated metal, into the hollows, causing the carved bone or shell to crack. The patterns of cracks, which resembled oracle script characters, provided the answer to the divination, though how they were interpreted is unknown.

Oracle bone script inscribed on a tortoise shell (Shang dynasty, c. 1766–1122 BCE).

SYMBOLS USED ON ORACLE BONES

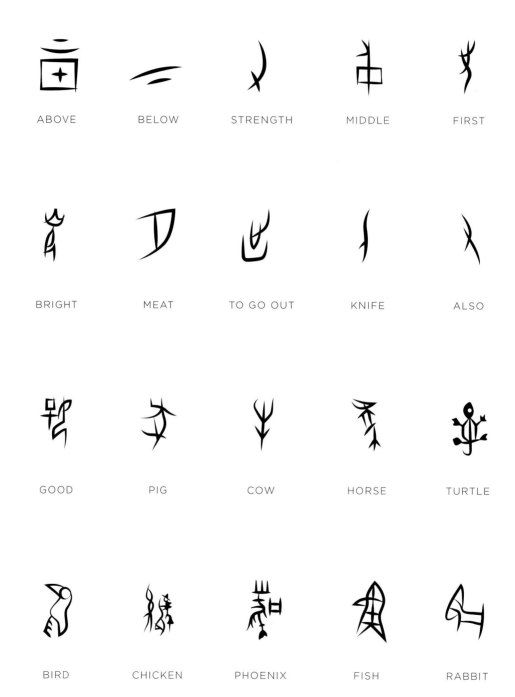

ABOVE	BELOW	STRENGTH	MIDDLE	FIRST
BRIGHT	MEAT	TO GO OUT	KNIFE	ALSO
GOOD	PIG	COW	HORSE	TURTLE
BIRD	CHICKEN	PHOENIX	FISH	RABBIT

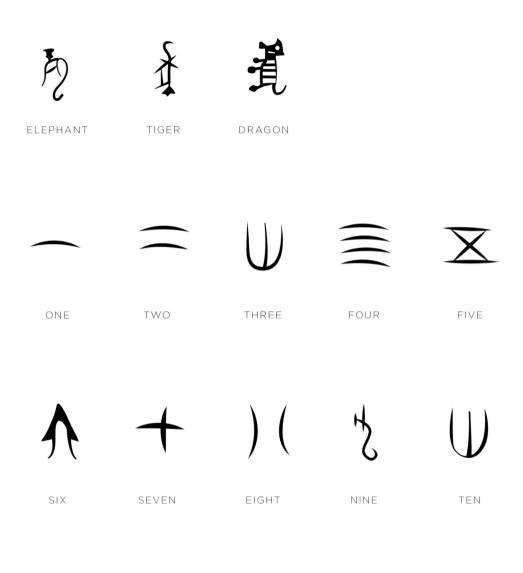

ELEPHANT   TIGER   DRAGON

ONE   TWO   THREE   FOUR   FIVE

SIX   SEVEN   EIGHT   NINE   TEN

HUNDRED   ONE THOUSAND   TEN THOUSAND

RONGORONGO

When Europeans first reached Rapa Nui in 1722, they were amazed and puzzled by what they found. They marvelled at the hundreds of giant stone *moai* and wondered how the impoverished population of a few thousand souls had built them on a desolate, barren island. For the islanders, Europeans brought nothing but disaster. By the 1860s, disease, civil strife, slaving raids and attacks by whalers had reduced the population to 111. Sadly, all those who knew their sacred lore and how to read the only script ever devised by Polynesians, Rongorongo, perished before passing on their secrets.

Although it would be easy to blame Europeans for the near extinction of the Rapa Nui, they themselves played a role in their own downfall. Their ancestors arrived on the island around the year 1200, making it one of the last places on Earth to be settled by humans. The handful of Polynesian mariners reached a lush, wooded paradise, rich in wildlife – a perfect home for weary travellers who had sailed 2,000 miles to get there. They decided to settle and became, in a very real sense, victims of their own success. They developed the extraordinary culture that sculpted and erected the giant moai and created the only Polynesian writing system, Rongorongo.

As their population swelled, the Rapa Nui began to exhaust the finite resources of the island: they drove its native animals to extinction and impoverished its soils. With no remaining trees to cut down to build ocean-going vessels, they were unable to leave the island that had become their prison. The arrival of European explorers in the eighteenth century, and of hostile whalers and Peruvian slavers in the nineteenth, merely hastened the collapse of a once thriving, dynamic culture.

In the twentieth century, the population and economy of the island revived – in recent years, largely as a result of tourism. But its traditional culture and the secrets of the Rongorongo glyphs, sadly, died with the last Rapa Nui elders, chiefs and ritual specialists. Rather than being passed down through generations, what is known of Rapa Nui history, culture and Rongorongo has been reconstructed by anthropologists, archaeologists and historians.

Above – A Birdman petroglyph at Orongo, Rapa Nui.

Opposite – A row of moai, the giant statues carved of volcanic stone, believed to memorialize important Rapa Nui chiefs.

RONGORONGO

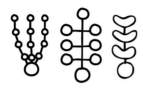

VARIOUS PLANTS

FRIGATE BIRD

SEA TURTLE

CATERPILLAR

CHEVRONS

MAN STANDING

SEATED MAN EATING

CRAYFISH

LOZENGES

PALM TREE

FISH

FLYING FISH

CENTIPEDE

CIRCLE

SQUID

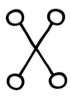

CROSS

MAYA GLYPHS

The classic Maya created the most sophisticated version of the Mesoamerican calendar and the only true writing system of signs, or glyphs, in the Americas, which they combined to produce vast libraries of books of natal divination and prophecy. Sadly, most of these were burned by the Spanish conquistadors in the sixteenth century in an attempt to eradicate Maya culture and religion. Fortunately, they did not succeed, and the Maya managed to preserve some of their traditional beliefs and divinatory practices.

The classic Maya, who lived in Mesoamerica between the third and tenth centuries CE, had two obsessions: blood and time. They believed that without sacrificial blood, the gods would perish, and the cosmos would be destroyed. Unlike the Aztecs of Mexico who had a democratic approach to human sacrifice, the Maya believed that the gods required royal blood. Thus, the Maya, rather than being the peace-loving, blissed-out astronomers of New Age accounts, were warriors who fought constant internecine warfare over scarce resources – the scarcest of all being the blood of royal captives. The timing of rituals and sacrifices was crucial to their efficacy, hence the need for an accurate calendar.

The Maya measured time obsessively because they believed that it was cyclical, and that past events would inevitably be repeated in the future. This did not mean just in the short term – in a few weeks, months or years – but across vast spans of time that went back into the distant past and far ahead into the distant future. Once such cycle of the Maya 'long count' began in 3114 BCE, said to be the date of the creation of the present age of the world, and ended in December 2012 – predicted by some occultists as the date of a cataclysm that would destroy the Earth. Despite much pseudoscientific and

Hollywood hype, we are still here, safe and sound, long after the expected disaster.

Another use of the Maya calendar was natal divination (see page 30). The 260-day ritual *Tzolk'in* calendar consisted of thirteen rounds of twenty days, each ruled by one of the guardians of the four cardinal points, K'an (yellow), Muluk (white), Ix (black) and Kawak (red). Each day was represented by an ideogram, or glyph, which, like the signs of Western astrology and the animal signs of the Chinese zodiac, was associated with certain characteristics. The circular nature of the periodization of Maya time meant that the calendar could also be used to predict the course of an individual's life.

IMIX',
THE ALLIGATOR

nurturing, east

IK',
THE WIND

versatility, north

AK'B'AL,
THE HOUSE

security, west

K'AN,
THE LIZARD

transition, south

CHIKCHAN,
THE SNAKE

transformation, east

KIMI,
DEATH

tradition, north

MANIK',
THE DEER

relationships, west

LAMAT,
THE RABBIT

adventure, south

MULUK,
WATER

emotion, east

OK, THE DOG
loyalty, north

CHUWEN, THE MONKEY
curiosity, west

EB', GRASS
healing, south

B'EN, REED
communication, east

IX, THE JAGUAR
power, north

MEN, THE EAGLE
vision, west

K'IB',
THE VULTURE

realism, south

KAB'AN, THE
EARTHQUAKE

movement, east

ETZ'NAB',
THE FLINT KNIFE

decision, north

KAWAK,
THE RAIN

renewal, west

AJAW,
THE FLOWER

fulfilment, south

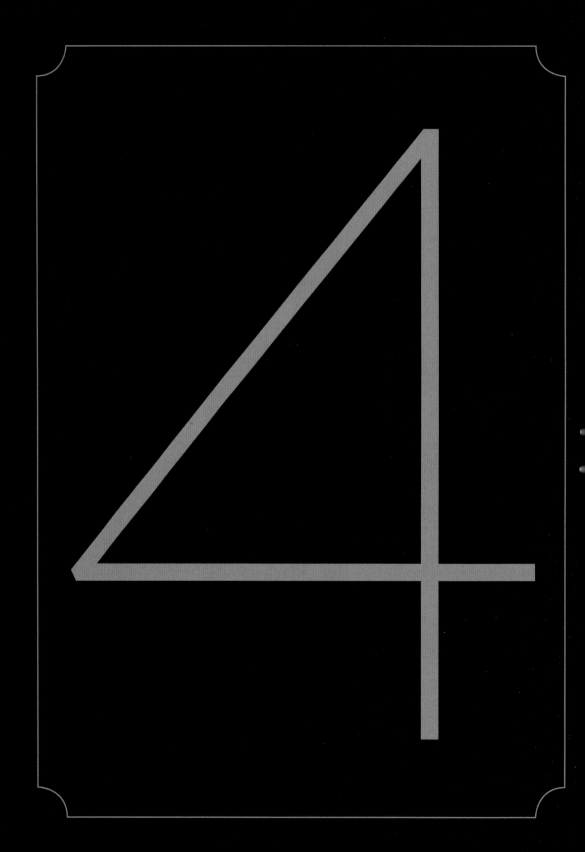

OCCULT
SCIENCES

———————————✶———————————

In premodern times, humans believed that they could
understand the purpose of the cosmos by discovering the
hidden knowledge encoded in nature. The techniques that
they developed to crack these codes would become the
occult sciences of alchemy, numerology, geomancy and
sacred geometry.

Curiosity is a characteristic we share with all primates. Even when it trumps caution, fear and common sense, curiosity is what makes humans the animal kingdom's most successful species. Prehistoric cave art suggests that the West's distant ancestors used magic to ensure success in the hunts on which they depended for survival. But as humans settled and their societies became ever more complex, so did their attempts to control the world through ritual and magic. Taking different routes, these developed into the occult sciences we will consider in this chapter.

Humans have always striven to understand the world and to answer the basic questions of existence. They have not pursued this knowledge for its own sake, but to control their fate in a dangerous and uncertain world. What had begun as the magical rituals of our nomadic hunter-gatherer ancestors who followed the herds of herbivores on which they depended for food, developed into the far more sophisticated ritual and magical practices of settled urban communities. The surplus provided by agriculture enabled the emergence of a class of ritual specialists who mediated the relationship between the gods and humanity and who engaged in the magical arts of medicine and metallurgy.

Gilgamesh, the hero of the Sumerian epic poem that bears his name, was the all-powerful king of the city of Uruk when he set off to seek the one thing denied him by the gods: the secret of immortality. His inevitable failure, and the lesson that he learned about coming to terms with death, did not discourage Chinese, Indian, Arab and Western alchemists from embarking on the same futile quest, often with fatal results for themselves and their royal patrons.

In order to control an increasingly complex world, you must first understand it. We saw in the previous chapter how the invention of writing provided a new way of describing and shaping the world, which, in turn, led to the emergence of a new script-based magic. In this chapter, we shall explore how humans used the occult sciences to decipher the hidden codes they identified in nature and natural phenomena.

Alchemists at work in the laboratory, showing the tools and equipment used during the medieval and early modern periods.

ALCHEMY

The ancient origins of alchemy can be found in the protoscientific corpus of writings concerned with the extraction and smelting of metals and the production of alloys and medicines. Though alchemy retained a relationship with technology, medicine and science until the eighteenth century, in its Western medieval and Renaissance iteration it was both a magical occult science pursuing the transmutation of base metals into gold and the creation of elixirs of immortality, and a spiritual discipline whose aims were the transformation of the soul and its union with the divine through the control of esoteric knowledge.

In the ancient world, there were three major traditions of alchemy: in China, India and the Greco-Roman Near East. Though their cultures were linked by the commercial network known as the 'Silk Road', they were independent of one another, as evidenced by their different conceptions of the elemental constituents of nature and human anatomy. What did link them was a shared interest in metallurgy and medicine, which were the two main alchemical pursuits of all three traditions.

With the end of antiquity, Chinese and Indian alchemy continued to develop uninterrupted, but in the Islamic world there was a new impetus caused by the Islamic conquest of Egypt and the Near East in the seventh century CE. Islamic alchemy (Arabic: *al-kimiyah*) inherited the corpus of philosophical, scientific and alchemical works of Hellenistic Egypt. Islamic alchemists systematized the practice of alchemy by stressing the importance of confirming theory with practical experimentation, which would, in time, become the basis of the modern scientific method.

Alchemy was introduced to the Christian West through Islamic Spain in the twelfth century, where the alchemical corpus had been combined with the Jewish Kabbalistic tradition that sought esoteric knowledge in scripture in order to attain a spiritual union with the divine that could not be gained through the prescribed ritual practices alone. This interpretation was initially embraced by the Catholic Church, which encouraged notions of spiritual alchemy paired with the search for the Philosopher's Stone that could transmute base metal into gold and grant immortality. But in the seventeenth century the Church turned against alchemy, forcing it underground. With its final separation from science during the Age of Enlightenment, alchemy became the domain of occultists who practised it as a pseudoscientific means of manipulating the physical world and as a transformational spiritual practice that rejected Christian doctrines.

HERMES TRISMEGISTUS

The purported founder of alchemy,
associated with the gods Hermes and Thoth.

THE CADUCEUS

Symbol of the Greek god Hermes and
of Western alchemy and medicine.

CHINESE ALCHEMY

Rather than seeking to transmute base metals into gold, Taoist alchemy focused on the development of medicines and the search for the elixir of immortality, which, however, did involve the use of metals, in particular mercury. A distinction was made between external, or *weidan*, alchemy, which employed substances from outside the human body; and *neidan*, which worked through internal practices, such as breathing techniques, exercise and meditation, to cultivate the life force, qi. Weidan elixirs of immortality often proved to be fatal because they were made from toxic substances. The first emperor of China, Shi Huang Di, who was obsessed with immortality, is said to have gone insane and died from ingesting an elixir containing mercury and powdered jade. Nevertheless, the Chinese alchemical tradition remains the basis for many traditional Chinese medical practices, such as herbology and acupuncture.

DAOIST MONK
A Daoist monk cultivating his qi in the lower abdomen, or *dantian*, to attain physical and spiritual immortality.

INDIAN ALCHEMY

Indian alchemy has its origins in the advanced metallurgy of ancient India, which was producing high-grade iron and steel centuries before they were successfully produced in Europe. As in Chinese, Islamic and Western alchemy, mercury was considered central to Indian practice, as evidenced by the Sanskrit term denoting alchemy: *rasaśāstra*, which means 'the science of mercury'. The fascination with the metal can be explained by mercury's unusual properties, being a liquid at ambient temperature and pressure. In traditional Ayurveda, toxic substances including mercury and arsenic were prescribed as cures, with predictably negative results. A reformed Ayurvedic pharmacopoeia, with the poisons removed (at least in the West), continues to follow the alchemical principles established by rasaśāstra.

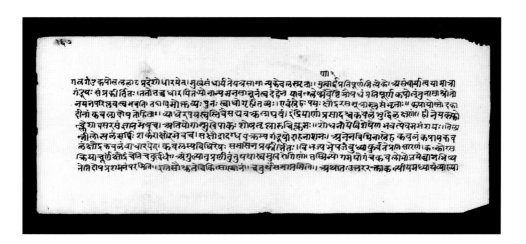

SANSKRIT
A page from the Sanskrit *Sushruta Samhita*
outlining the principles of Ayurvedic medicine.

ISLAMIC ALCHEMY

Islamic alchemy inherited the Greco-Egyptian alchemical corpus when Arab armies conquered Egypt in the seventh century CE. Although Hellenistic Egypt had been part of the Christian Eastern Roman, or Byzantine, Empire for centuries before the Muslim conquest, its alchemists looked back to Egypt's pagan pharaonic past and to the advanced metallurgy and alchemy that they believed had been developed by the ancient Egyptian priesthood. The major contribution of Islamic scholars was the systematization of the theory and practice of classical alchemy.

Islam inherited a confused corpus of Greek philosophical, Pythagorean, alchemical and Gnostic texts, dating from the early centuries of the Common Era, known as the *Hermetica* after its purported author, the mythical Hermes Trismegistus (Thrice-Great Hermes). He was said to have been a contemporary of Moses, and was identified with the ancient Egyptian god of Wisdom, Thoth, and the Greek god, Hermes, whose staff, the caduceus, became the symbol of Western alchemy and medicine.

We owe the term 'alchemy' to Islamic scholarship, which first called it *al-kimiyah* in the tenth century CE. Interest in alchemy developed soon after the conquest of Egypt. In the seventh century, Prince Khalid ibn Yazid (known in the West as Calid) instigated the translation of the Hermetic corpus into Arabic, making it available to Islamic scholars. In the next two centuries, Abū Mūsā Jābir ibn Ḥayyān and Abū Bakr Muhammad ibn Zakariyā al-Rāzī, known in the West as Geber and Rhazes, retrospectively systematized its study and practice. In order to obtain true mastery, Geber explained, al-kimiyah had to be put on a sound scientific basis, which meant testing the confused Greco-Egyptian alchemical theories with laboratory-based experiments whose results could be duplicated. Although Geber's aims, like those of all alchemists, were pseudoscientific, his systematic approach to the discipline and his discoveries have earned him the epithet 'father of chemistry'.

Al-kimiyah's achievements display the typical alchemical mix of practical discoveries – such as *aqua regia*, a potent compound of hydrochloric and nitric acids that could dissolve metals including gold, platinum and mercury – and pseudoscientific theories of matter, such as the pairing of the qualities of heat, cold, wetness and dryness with the four classical elements, whose manipulation, it was believed, could transmute base metals into 'noble' ones. This provided the basis for the holy grail of Western alchemy, the quest for the Philosopher's Stone – a hypothetical substance thought to grant immortality and change base metals into gold or silver.

A Western portrait of Abū Mūsā Jābir ibn Ḥayyān, known in the West as Geber.

MEDIEVAL & RENAISSANCE ALCHEMY

Despite its Islamic origins, alchemy was initially welcomed by the Catholic Church, becoming an established Christian practice by the thirteenth century. However, the Church's benign attitude did not last. Challenged by Renaissance humanism and the Protestant Reformation, the Catholic Church moved against all heterodox beliefs and practices. Alchemy, with its associations with magic and astrology, and already tarnished by accusations of charlatanism, was proscribed. Alchemists were imprisoned and burned as heretics. During the Enlightenment, the emerging scientific establishment consciously distanced itself from its alchemical origins.

The five centuries after alchemy's introduction to Western Europe through Muslim Spain witnessed a tripartite fight over its soul, between religion, science and occultism. The medieval Church was firmly in charge of scholarship and at first encouraged the study of works of alchemy that had been translated from Arabic. At a time when divination and astrology were not considered to contradict church teaching, alchemy was readily accepted. This led to the development of Christian alchemical and kabbalistic traditions (the latter derived from the supposed writings of the legendary Hermes Trismegistus; see page 230) which combined the search for the Philosopher's Stone and a cure-all panacea with a spiritual alchemy of Christian salvation.

Once the Catholic and Protestant churches had turned against alchemy, practitioners withdrew to the safety of secret societies, where they could teach and practise their art more or less unmolested. In the eighteenth century, natural scientists, astronomers and doctors, who had once found a home within the alchemical tradition, consciously broke away to establish their own learned societies, leaving the pursuit of pseudoscientific alchemy to occultists and charlatans.

Alchemy shares many of its symbols with astrology, which shows the close links between the two pseudosciences. Not only do the symbols represent a handy notation system, but they were also adopted to keep alchemical secrets, as well as to endow alchemy with a veneer of occult esoteric knowledge. In response to this deliberate obscurantism, scientists developed entirely new systems of notation for chemistry, physics and mathematics.

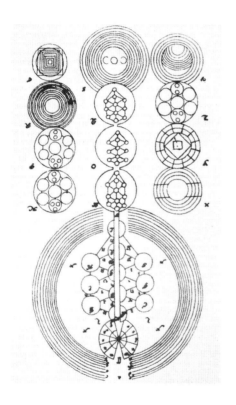

THE *SEFIROT*

The *sefirot* (emanations), from *Kabbala Denudata* by Christian Knorr von Rosenroth (1636–89), a Christian interpretation of the Jewish mystical Kabbalah.

ALCHEMICAL SYMBOLS

Table of alchemical symbols from *The Last Will and Testament* attributed to the sixteenth-century German monk Basil Valentine (possibly a pseudonym).

THE FOUR CLASSICAL ELEMENTS

There was no agreement among the ancient Greeks about the number and nature of the classical elements. The five elements given in Chapter 2 (page 36) represent the Aristotelian theory of matter, which was not universally accepted in antiquity or the Middle Ages. Aristotle's teacher, Plato, favoured four elements that he associated with colours, qualities and the sacred geometric forms known as Platonic solids. The fifth-century CE Greek philosopher Democritus theorized that matter was composed of different kinds of 'atoms' too small to see with the naked eye, which proved to be much closer to the modern scientific understanding of the chemical elements.

FIRE
red or orange, masculine, hot and dry. Red is the colour of blood, associated with male aggression.

EARTH
green or brown, cold and dry. Associated with the colours of the soil and vegetation.

AIR
white, blue or grey, hot and wet. The upward triangle indicates the rising nature of air.

WATER
blue, feminine, cold and wet. The inverted triangle reflects the descending nature of water.

TRIA PRIMA

In the eighth century the Islamic alchemist Geber added two new elements, mercury and sulphur, respectively symbols of the properties of metal and combustibility, to the four classical elements. The sixteenth-century Swiss alchemist and physician Paracelsus added a third new substance, salt, creating the concept of the three primes, or *tria prima*, to which he ascribed the causes and cures of all diseases. He did not describe sulphur, mercury and salt as elements in their own right but as the three metallic principles acting on the four classical elements, which had both chemical and spiritual properties.

MERCURY

The symbol of the planet Mercury and of metallic mercury (quicksilver), representing volatility. As one of the three primes, it stood for the eternal life force. Composed of a cross and the symbol for Taurus.

SULPHUR

The symbol for sulphur was the intermediary between the two other primes of mercury and salt. It represented combustibility and flammability, evaporation and dissolution. Composed of a cross and the triangle symbolizing fire.

SALT

Although no longer recognized as a chemical element but as a compound, salt is essential to life. In the tria prima, salt represented solidity, condensation and crystallization, and in a broader sense, the underlying essence of the physical body. Represented as a bisected circle.

SILVER

IRON

QUICKSILVER

TIN

COPPER

LEAD

GOLD

THE PLANETARY METALS

The seven planetary metals were each assigned a celestial 'ruler', which in medieval and Renaissance astronomy and astrology meant the Sun and Moon and the five known planets, Mercury, Venus, Mars, Jupiter and Saturn. Each heavenly body was also associated with a part of the body, a day of the week and a number of medicinal herbs. For example, Venus ruled the kidneys; thus, its associated herbs, thyme, mint, greater burdock, althaea, motherwort and plantain, were thought beneficial for renal complaints. Listed below are the symbols for the seven planetary metals, each with its ruler, part of the body and a sample of two herbal remedies.

SILVER

Crescent Moon, Monday, brain, hyssop and white willow. Represented as a crescent to differentiate it from the Sun.

IRON

Mars, Tuesday, gallbladder, gentian and garlic. The arrow symbolizes phallic masculinity and weaponry.

QUICKSILVER

Mercury, Wednesday, lungs, verbena and valerian. The changeling metal that is solid as an ore and liquid in its pure form.

TIN

Jupiter, Thursday, liver, dandelion and oak. A constituent of bronze, tin is represented by a stylized number four.

COPPER

Venus, Friday, kidneys, thyme and mint. Combined with tin to make bronze, copper was the first metal exploited by humans.

LEAD

Saturn, Saturday, spleen, fumewort and shepherd's purse. An environmental poison, lead was represented by a stylized letter H with cross.

GOLD

Sun, Sunday, heart, chamomile and celandine. Also represented by a circle with a central dot, gold was held by some cultures to be the 'sweat' of the Sun.

THE MUNDANE ELEMENTS

Alchemists identified a number of 'mundane' elements, which they believed to be made up of the four classical elements, but that coincidentally correspond to modern chemical elements found on the periodic table. They used the mundane elements in the course of their quest to find the Philosopher's Stone and the Universal Panacea, and did not realize the true significance of their accidental discoveries. Each of these elements was assigned a symbol designed to impress and mystify the uninitiated. Certain elements were associated with animals in a symbolic mnemonic system similar to that used in the Chinese zodiac.

ANTIMONY

Antimony represents humanity's wild or animal nature and is sometimes symbolized by the wolf. The symbol is an upside-down version of the planet Venus.

ARSENIC

Arsenic is a metalloid element that can transform its appearance. Although known to be a poison, it was associated with the swan, which transmutes from an unattractive cygnet into the graceful adult bird. The symbol is made up of two interlocked triangles.

BISMUTH

Bismuth's uses in alchemy are not well understood, and until the eighteenth century it was often confused with other elements such as tin or lead. The symbol is the same as that used for Taurus.

MAGNESIUM

Magnesium is not found in its pure form in nature; alchemists used it in the compound magnesium carbonate, a white anhydrous salt that they called *magnesium alba*. The symbol is a bisected letter D.

PHOSPHORUS

Phosphorus appears to have the ability to hold light, because white phosphorus glows green when it oxidizes. It represented the spirit. Inflammable phosphorus contains the element fire.

PLATINUM

Platinum was believed to be a combination of gold and silver as opposed to a separate metallic element, which is why its symbol combines those for the Sun and Moon. The symbol is the Moon crescent combined with the Sun disc.

POTASSIUM

Potassium doesn't exist as an element in nature and alchemists used the compound potassium carbonate, or potash. The symbol is a cross topped by a rectangle.

ZINC

Zinc was burned by alchemists to produce zinc oxide, *nix alba*, 'white snow' or 'philosopher's wool'. The symbol is a letter Z with an additional vertical stroke.

ALCHEMICAL COMPOUNDS & UNITS

In their quest to discover the Philosopher's Stone and the Universal Panacea, alchemists developed complex techniques that required laboratories, equipment, furnaces and reagents to manipulate the materia prima, the base matter that they selected to transmute. To keep their work secret from their rivals, they created an alchemical notation of abstract signs for reagents, alcohols, alloys and units of time and measurement.

SAL AMMONIAC

(ammonium chloride) is named after the Egyptian sun god Amun-Ra.

AQUA FORTIS

(nitric acid) was first discovered by Islamic alchemists.

AQUA REGIA

(nitro-hydrochloric acid) was used by Islamic alchemists to dissolve gold, silver and platinum.

AQUA VITAE

is a concentrated aqueous solution of ethanol, also known as spirits of wine.

AMALGAM

is an alloy of mercury with another metal.

CINNABAR

(mercury sulphide) is the main source for elemental mercury.

VITRIOL

refers to the crystalline sulphates of various metals that occur in different colours.

UNITS

HOUR

3 3β

DRAM AND
HALF-DRAM

3 3β

OUNCE AND
HALF-OUNCE

SCRUPLE

℔

POUND

MAGNUM OPUS & THE PHILOSOPHER'S STONE

The Magnum Opus (Great Work) of alchemy is the quest for the Philosopher's Stone, the substance said to be able to transmute base metals into the noble metals silver, gold and platinum, and to grant immortal life. For the followers of spiritual alchemy, this meant the successive degrees of spiritual purification and the attainment of salvation and union with Godhead through esoteric means. Initially there were three or four stages in the Magnum Opus, but these were later increased to seven, twelve or fourteen different stages that corresponded to the manipulation of base matter (materia prima) or to the passage through different stages of initiation in a spiritual journey. The symbols used in the twelve-stage Magnum Opus shown here are those of the Western zodiac.

TWELVE STAGES OF THE MAGNUM OPUS

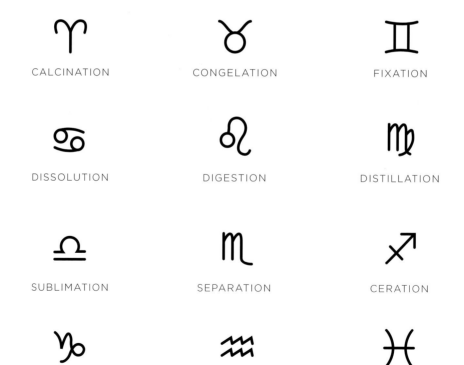

♈	♉	♊
CALCINATION	CONGELATION	FIXATION
♋	♌	♍
DISSOLUTION	DIGESTION	DISTILLATION
♎	♏	♐
SUBLIMATION	SEPARATION	CERATION
♑	♒	♓
FERMENTATION	MULTIPLICATION	PROJECTION

THE PHILOSOPHER'S STONE

This symbol began to be used during the seventeenth
century. It is made up of circles, squares and triangles
that represent the four elements of matter that form
the Philosopher's Stone.

OTHER ALCHEMICAL SYMBOLS

Obsessed with preserving their secrets from the prying eyes of rivals, and determined to impress the uninitiated and gullible, alchemists devised symbols to represent every aspect of their pseudoscience, including its basic elements, processes and all the materials needed for its practice. This section features the everyday substances which alchemists represented with pictograms and abstract symbols.

SAND

SOAP

VINEGAR

VERDIGRIS

URINE

REALGAR

OIL

GUM

SAL ALKALI

ASHES

CRYSTAL

TALLOW

CAMPHIRE

WAX

HARTSHORN

CERUSE

NUMEROLOGY

We might ask ourselves which came first: pictograms or numbers? But logic dictates that they must have been invented at the same time, because when ancient scribes impressed pictograms for cattle, sheep and bushels of grain onto clay tokens, they had to indicate how many of each were in the shipment. Like ideograms, hieroglyphs and letters, numbers were a new way of representing the world, and soon they too became the basis for new forms of divination and magic through which humans sought to control it.

When humans lived in small bands of hunter-gatherers, all they needed to count, add and subtract were their ten fingers. But our ancestors did not stick to the decimal or vigesimal system (if you add the toes), because nature does not usually work in tens. After they had become settled agriculturalists, humans needed ever more sophisticated numbers and numerical operations to manage the complexities of their emerging urban civilizations. In order to measure time and plot the movements of the heavens, the Babylonians devised the sexagesimal system, which explains why there are sixty minutes in an hour, and why the angles of a triangle always add up to 360 degrees.

Numbers gave humans another tool to understand the world and seek to control it. Ancient Greek and Hebrew used the same symbols for the letters of the alphabet and for numbers, creating a ready-made link that became the basis for the numerological techniques of Greek isopsephy and Hebrew gematria (both of which involve counting up the numerical values of the letters in a word). A leading exponent of numerology, the ancient Greek mathematician Pythagoras, was the first to discover the relationship between musical notes and numbers. In addition to assigning symbolic meanings

to the numerals one to seven, he devised the system that assigned numerical values to individual letters. His system was widely adopted in antiquity and the Middle Ages. The Islamic alchemist Geber, though wedded to scientific experimentation, framed his work according to complex numerological relationships between the names of substances in Arabic.

Other important numerological traditions include the East Asian belief that certain numbers are lucky or unlucky, according to their occurrence on a calendar, whether they are odd or even, or because they are homophones of words with negative associations. Another type of numerology unique to East Asia is assigning an occult significance to the number of strokes used to write the characters of a person's name.

Different ways to render numbers in written script. The numbers one to five often resemble stylized fingers and a hand.

	Cuneiform	Egyptian	Chinese	Latin	Arabic
1	𒁹	١	一	I	١
2	𒈫	�|	二	II	٢
3	 𒐈	 �	三	III	٣
4	 𒐉	 �	四	IV	٤
5	𒐊	٦	五	V	٥
6	𒐋	 ٧	六	VI	٦
7	 𒐌	 ٢	七	VII	٧
8	𒐍	 ٢	八	VIII	٨
9	𒐎	 ٢	九	IX	٩
10	𒌋	٨	十	X	١٠

ISOPSEPHY & GEMATRIA

Greek isopsephy and Hebrew gematria study the connections between words that have the same numerical values as calculated according to the upper table shown opposite. Adapted for their own use by Islamic scholars, these numerological techniques attempted to uncover occult links between names, events and ideas. One of the best known of these associations is the Number of the Beast from the biblical Book of Revelation.

666

St John of Patmos wrote the Book of Revelation around 96 CE, and in the intervening 1,900 years occultists have been trying to identify the person designated by the Number of the Beast. It is likely that every major world leader from the emperor Nero to Adolf Hitler and beyond has been linked with the figure of the Antichrist whose birth on Earth heralds Armageddon and the Day of Judgment. Roman emperors were early targets, in particular Nero, whose persecution of Christians was said to have been particularly bloodthirsty. But depending on how his name was styled, as either *Neron Caesar* or *Nero Caesar*, the gematria number was different: 666 with the *n* or 616 without it. Ultimately, the Church fathers chose 666, which, it must be admitted, looks and sounds a lot more sinister than the rather bland 616.

ONOMANCY

Numerology based on a person's given name is known as 'onomancy'. In the Pythagorean and Babylonian systems, the letters of the alphabet were distributed among the numbers one to nine according to the lower table shown opposite. A refinement of the system also obtains a number from the person's date of birth. The letters are added up until a single digit is obtained and interpreted according to the system used. Different numbers are said to reveal different aspects of the self, and also allow for the working out of lucky times of day or lucky years.

The name Nero Claudius Caesar yields the number 9, while his birth date of 15 December 37 CE yields the number 1.

DECIMAL	HEBREW	ARABIC	GREEK
1	א	أ	A α
2	ב	ب	B β
3	ג	ج	Γ γ
4	ד	د	Δ δ
5	ה	ه	E ε
6	ו	و	ϛ' Ϝ
7	ז	ز	Z ζ
8	ח	ح	H η
9	ט	ط	Θ θ
10	י	ي	I ι
20	כ	ك	K κ
30	ל	ل	Λ λ
40	מ	م	M μ
50	נ	ن	N ν
60	ס	س	ξ ξ
70	ע	ع	o o
80	פ	ف	π π
90	צ	ص	Ϙ'
100	ק	ق	ρ ρ
200	ר	ر	σ σ
300	ש	ش	τ τ
400	ת	ت	υ υ
500	ך	ث	φ φ
600	ם	خ	χ χ
700	ן	ذ	ψ ψ
800	ף	ض	Ω
900	ץ	ظ	ϡ'

1	2	3	4	5	6	7	8	9
a	b	c	d	e	f	g	h	i
j	k	l	m	n	o	p	q	r
s	t	u	v	w	x	y	z	

LUCKY & UNLUCKY NUMBERS

The meaning of numbers and whether they are considered lucky or unlucky varies widely across cultures and historical periods. Pythagoras is thought to have established the first systematic numerology in the ancient world, influenced by his mathematical and geometrical discoveries. Pythagorean numerology was elaborated into more complicated systems during the medieval period. A quite distinct set of associations making a number lucky or unlucky is found in East Asia, though there is no exact agreement on the status of numbers even among neighbouring cultures.

PYTHAGOREAN NUMBERS

A

ONE

unity, representing the divine that is not divisible into smaller parts.

B

TWO

diversity and disorder, the principle of opposition and evil; also the female number.

Γ

THREE

harmony, representing the union of 1 and 2, unity and diversity; also the male number.

Δ

FOUR

cosmos; a significant number because it is the first square (2 x 2).

E

FIVE

The union of the female and male numbers is symbolic of partnership.

7

Seven is considered to be the luckiest number, and is regularly voted people's favourite number, though it is unclear why this should be, unless it can be explained by the sevens in everyday life (days of the week, ages of man, etc.).

63

In medieval numerology, the numbers seven and nine and their odd multiples (21, 27, 35, 49, 63, 81) were thought to be particularly unlucky, especially 7 x 9 = 63, known as the 'grand climacteric number', an age that few people in the medieval period reached.

13

In Norse mythology, during a feast attended by twelve of the Aesir, the uninvited god Loki kills one of the guests – an event echoed in the more usual explanation for the number being considered unlucky as the number of guests present at the Last Supper.

Eight is considered the luckiest number in China because it is a homophone for the word 'prosperity'. Eighty-eight is doubly lucky because it's a homophone for 'double happiness'.

Shi or *si* is a homophone for 'death' in Chinese, Japanese and Korean. You might not find a room four or a fourth floor in a Chinese hotel, and other numbers containing four, such as fourteen and seventy-four, are avoided because they are homophones for 'is dead' and 'is already dead'.

In Japan it is the number nine, *ku*, that is considered the unluckiest as it is a homophone for the words 'pain' and 'suffering'. In contrast, nine is considered lucky in China because of its associations with longevity and eternity.

| | 25 | 42 | 61 |
| MEN | 二十五 | 四十二 | 六十一 |

| | 19 | 33 | 37 |
| WOMEN | 十九 | 三十三 | 三十七 |

Ages that are considered particularly unlucky in Japan are known as *honyaku*: for men (upper row) these are 25, 42 and 61, and for women, 19, 33 and 37. To ward off misfortune, a person reaching those ages might go to a Shinto shrine to perform purification rites.

SACRED GEOMETRY

When our distant ancestors began to draw geometric patterns, they made a fundamental cognitive leap. We shall never know what the patterns meant to them, but the creation of abstract symbols is evidence that they had mastered a form of reasoning that has never been demonstrated in any other animal species. In the succeeding millennia, humans laid out megalithic monuments and buildings in geometric patterns aligned with the cardinal points or with the positions of celestial bodies and determined by geomantic and occult principles. At their most idealized, geometric forms have been used to describe the constituents of matter and to create visual representations of the cosmos.

It was once thought that archaic humans became fully sapient around 40,000 years ago, when they started to decorate caves in Europe with painted and incised images of animals. But recent discoveries have pushed the cognitive developments associated with behavioural modernity further and further back in time. The topmost image on the facing page is the first known abstract pattern made by humans. It was discovered in the Blombos Cave in Cape Province, South Africa, and dates back 73,000 years. The pattern scratched on a piece of rock is not drawn with the exactitude of a modern draughtsman working with a ruler and protractor, but it is recognizably a set of interlocked triangles and lozenges – forms that do not exist in nature.

The Blombos ochre fragment represents the first known example of the geometrical figures and abstract patterns that have been found in prehistoric sites all over the world. We can be sure that they are not clumsy attempts at representing concrete objects because our ancestors were extraordinarily talented draughtsmen, as evidenced by the representations of animals in the Lascaux and Altamira caves. Therefore, they may represent something that does not have a physical form, possibly such concepts as death, divinity, the soul or the afterlife.

In the construction of megalithic monuments, such as Stonehenge (opposite, middle image) and Carnac, the alignment, configuration and shapes of the stones were all carefully chosen, establishing principles of sacred geometry that would be applied to the layout of the temple complex of Angkor Wat (opposite, lower image), and to the depiction of abstract occult, magical, divinatory and cosmological concepts in diagrammatic form.

Incised ochre rock from Blombos, South Africa, c. 73,000 years BP (c. 71,000 BCE).

Stonehenge, Wiltshire, England, c. 3000 BCE.

Angkor Wat, Cambodia, c. 1110–50 CE.

TETRACTYS

The tetractys was the main symbol of Pythagoreanism, used in its cultic initiation ceremonies and the swearing-in of new members. The diagram is made up of ten points, representing the cardinal numbers one to ten, which, when joined, form nine interlocking equilateral triangles that are reminiscent of the design scratched in the Blombos Cave around 72,000 years earlier. They, in turn, constitute a larger equilateral triangle, whose ten points and four rows represent the occult connections established between musical notation, numbers and geometrical forms that are the basis for the cosmological beliefs espoused by Pythagoras and his followers.

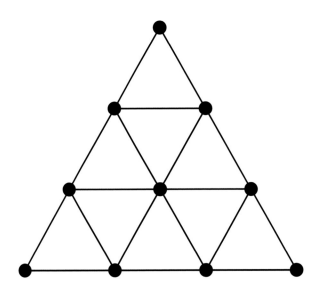

PLATONIC SOLIDS

The ancient Greek philosopher Plato proposed that what exists in the reality that we are able to experience with our senses is an imperfect reflection of a spiritual dimension of perfect 'forms', which we can conceive of but never apprehend directly. In the same vein, in his fourth-century BCE philosophical dialogue *Timaeus*, Plato suggested a direct association between the five classical elements and ideal geometric solids – the five Platonic solids – chosen to reflect the physical properties of each element. He linked earth with the cube, air with the octahedron, water with the icosahedron, fire with the tetrahedron and aether with the dodecahedron.

TETRAHEDRON

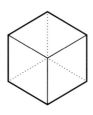

CUBE

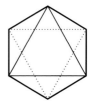

OCTAHEDRON

DODECAHEDRON

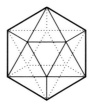

ICOSAHEDRON

MANDALAS & YANTRAS

Mandalas and yantras are pictorial representations of cosmological concepts constructed from ideal geometric forms, which are used in the esoteric tantric traditions of Hinduism and Buddhism. Mandalas are particularly prominent in Tibetan Buddhism. Yantras are used in Hindu rituals (*puja*) and meditation (*dhyana*) to focus the mind. Whereas mandalas are two-dimensional designs painted on scrolls and walls, or made out of coloured sand and erased at the end of the ritual, yantras can also be made into three-dimensional objects made of stone, wood or metal.

A mandala represents both the whole cosmos and the stages through which a devotee must pass to attain spiritual liberation from the cycle of life, death and rebirth, and enlightenment. A Tibetan mandala is a symbolic space that a meditator visualizes and imagines entering as if he were walking into a physical location. Beginning at the outer edges of the mandala, he must cross two outer circles – one of flames and the second of *vajra* (ritual weapons). Within the circle is a square representing the 'pure palace', whose four walls, decorated with auspicious symbols, are pierced with four entrances corresponding to the cardinal points. The divinities within symbolize the spiritual emanations of the central figure of the Buddha, with whom the meditator identifies, in a process that sees his body, mind and spirit merge with the mandala.

Yantras are geometric designs that represent the cosmos and specific Hindu deities that are each associated with a pattern. A yantra is a visual equivalent of a mantra, the sacred sound used in meditation and chanting. When a mantra is laid upon a yantra it is invested with the power of its specific deity. The most powerful yantra is Sri yantra, which consists of nine intersecting triangles – five representing Shakti and four representing Siva, respectively the female and male principles. These are surrounded by five circles embellished with lotus petals, and three concentric rectangles with four gates. While yantras are intended to be used as a means to reach enlightenment, they can also serve much baser magical purposes such as protection, fulfilling desires, controlling others and killing enemies.

Above — A three-dimensional metal yantra of Mount Meru.

Opposite — A Tibetan mandala representing the Buddhist cosmos as arrangements of circles and squares containing images of the various Vajra Buddhas.

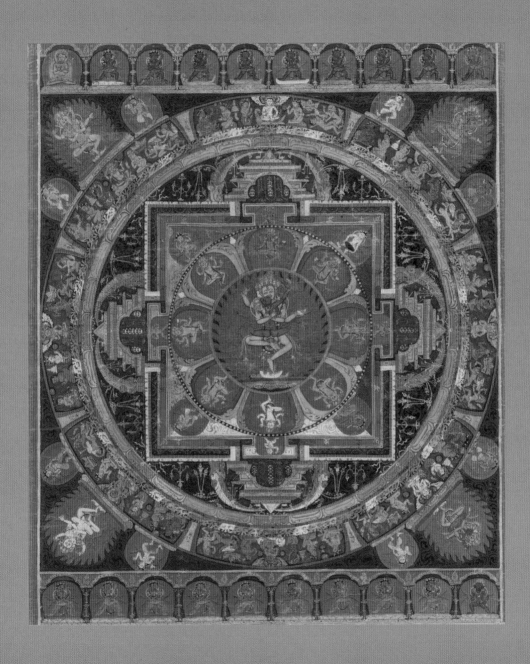

YANTRAS

KAMALA YANTRA

BUBANESHWARA
YANTRA

TARA YANTRA

BAGALA-MUKHI
YANTRA

MATANGI YANTRA

TRIPURA-
SUNDARI YANTRA

DURGA YANTRA

KALI YANTRA

GANESHA
YANTRA

SIVA YANTRA

SRI CHAKRA
YANTRA

SRI YANTRA

FENG SHUI LUOPAN

Readers may be familiar with the network of ley lines that criss-cross the countryside linking sacred sites such as Stonehenge and Glastonbury, which are said to transmit spiritual energy. Chinese geomancy, feng shui (literally 'wind and water'), is an occult science that has systematized the same principles, seeking to harmonize the flow of the subtle energy, qi, around the landscape and within cities and buildings to maximize health, harmony and good fortune. The luopan is a geomantic compass oriented with the South Pole that consists of up to forty concentric rings representing the basic concepts of Chinese cosmology.

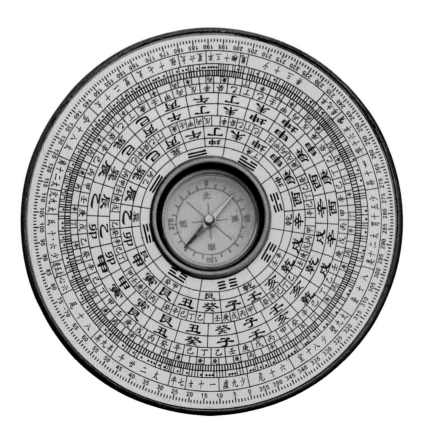

TIANTAN

It took fourteen years (1406–20) to landscape and build the huge Temple of Heaven complex in Beijing, of which the Tiantan, or Altar of Heaven, forms part. The site was carefully chosen and laid out, following geomantic feng shui principles, to stage the ceremony on the winter solstice when the emperor stepped onto the Altar of Heaven, which was a physical representation of the Chinese cosmos, to perform a ritual believed to ensure the peace and prosperity of the empire for the coming year. The Tiantan consists of elements arranged in nines or multiples of nine: three circular terraces with three sets of staircases at the cardinal points; the upper platform is laid out in nine concentric circles of marble paving slabs, with eighty-one outer stones and 360 balustrade supports corresponding to the 360 degrees of a geometric circle.

WHITE MAGIC & CARTOMANCY

White magic is that part of the Western occult tradition
that sought to work within the tenets of Christianity for
the betterment and salvation of humanity, to which can be
added eighteenth-century cartomancy – fortune-telling
using playing cards or the Tarot – which was seen as a
harmless form of popular entertainment.

From the perspective of the twenty-first century, occultism and magic must exist in opposition to the beliefs and rituals of revealed religion. We have the example of Moses defeating Pharaoh's magicians in the Old Testament, alongside any other number of examples that demonstrate the superiority of divine power over the demoniacal magic of the devil and pagan gods. But in the early modern mind, there existed a tradition of what may be called white magic, precisely evidenced by the miraculous feats performed by God, his angels and prophets and his only begotten son, Jesus Christ.

In order to understand white magic, we must imagine a world that is not explained by scientific rationality but by the scriptural revelations of the Old and New Testaments, which in themselves encapsulate quite different world views: Jewish and Christian. These are often at odds, because in the Jewish interpretation the Messiah is yet to come, and his coming will bring about the end of the world, while the Christian revelation accepts that Jesus as the Messiah has deferred the end of the world to an indeterminate future Day of Judgment.

Medieval and Renaissance occultism absorbed the Jewish esoteric spirituality of the Kabbalah, which it had Christianized by changing its spelling to 'Cabala', but which created an intellectual rift with orthodox Christian teaching that gave occultists permission to explore magical and occult practices that were not sanctioned by the Church. Importantly, nor were they proscribed, because when they were first introduced, they were not seen as antithetical to Christian revelation. The grandees of the medieval Church were interested in the possibilities, material,

political and spiritual, of the occult sciences of alchemy and astrology. During the Renaissance, scholars such as Johannes Trithemius, Heinrich Cornelius Agrippa and John Dee did not see magic as an impious collaboration with demonic forces. They believed in the existence, in parallel with demonology and necromancy, of a form of occultism that could be used for the betterment of humanity and its spiritual advancement towards salvation. Of course, there was a fine line between white and black magic, which occultists sometimes consciously chose to cross.

During the eighteenth-century Enlightenment, Christian revelation had lost its absolute hold, allowing for a new form of occultism and magic to emerge as entertainment with the use of playing cards and the Tarot.

The Archangel Michael Defeating Satan *by Lucas Kilian, 1588.*

S · MICHAEL ·
Archangelus ·

OPVS EX ÆRE
EFFBERT·GER-
HOLA·ALTIT
PEDV XIV

CANDID.
LINEAVIT·
OELER EXC
ENETIIS

MAGNO·PRINCIPI· GVILIELMO ·V· COM·PALAT· RHENI, VTRIVSᵩ BAVARIAE·DVCI·
BASILICÆ·D·MICHAELIS·ARCHANGELI·APVD·MONACENSES, AMPLISS·ÆTERN·CONDITO·

THE THEBAN ALPHABET

The letters of the Theban alphabet, also known as the alphabet of Honorius, correspond exactly to those of the ancient Latin alphabet, indicating its possible use as a cipher to transliterate Latin text. Theban first appeared in the works of a sixteenth-century occultist, and like other magical alphabets and ciphers of the period, its origins are deliberately obscure and its attribution almost certainly invented. The script itself is unique, but its letters resemble astrological and alchemical symbols of the same period.

The Theban alphabet is attributed to Honorius of Thebes, of whom nothing is known apart from his presumed authorship of a medieval grimoire (book of magic), *The Sworn Book of Honorius,* written in the thirteenth or fourteenth century. The soubriquet 'of Thebes' endows Honorius with a spurious antiquity, associating him with either the ancient Egyptian capital of Thebes, held in the Renaissance to be one of the centres of magic, or with the similarly exotic ancient Greek town of the same name. However, the Theban alphabet is not found in *The Sworn Book of Honorius* but makes its first appearance in the writings of the Benedictine abbot and occultist Johannes Trithemius (1462–1516).

Trithemius, born Johannes Heidenberg, ran away from home aged seventeen, because his stepfather had banned him from studying. Possessing an impressive intellect, he took holy orders and studied at the University of Heidelberg. Upon graduation, aged twenty-one, he became the abbot of the Benedictine Abbey of Sponheim, which he determined to turn into a centre of learning. His reputation as an occultist led to his resignation, but he was offered another abbey in Würzburg where he spent the remaining years of his life. His students included the occultist

Heinrich Cornelius Agrippa von Nettesheim and the alchemist and doctor Paracelsus.

The Theban alphabet first appeared in Trithemius' *Polygraphia,* published posthumously in 1518, and reappeared in the work of his student Heinrich Cornelius Agrippa. It seems unlikely that the true creator of the script was the mythical Honorius of Thebes, nor, as has also been suggested, the seventh-century Pope Honorius I or the thirteenth-century Pope Honorius III. (The attribution of the alphabet to the papacy is probably due to much later Protestant hostility to Roman Catholicism.) The alphabet has since found favour among the practitioners of Wicca.

Johannes Trithemius, who may have created the Theban alphabet.

THE THEBAN ALPHABET

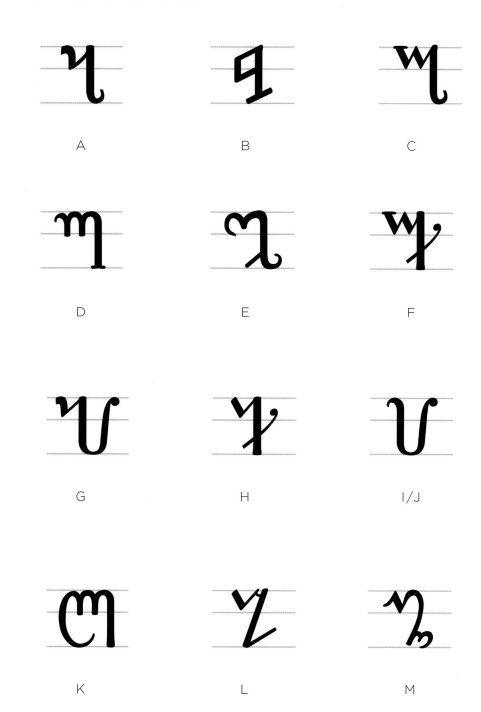

A

B

C

D

E

F

G

H

I/J

K

L

M

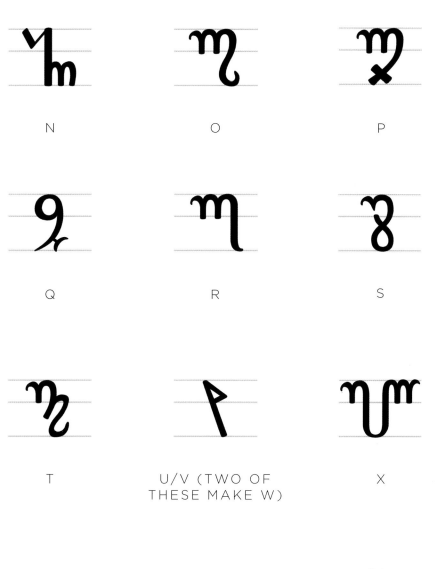

N

O

P

Q

R

S

T

U/V (TWO OF
THESE MAKE W)

X

Y

Z

END OF
SENTENCE

SCRIPTS FROM *DE OCCULTA PHILOSOPHIA*

The three alphabetic scripts known as 'Malachim', 'Celestial' and 'Passing of the River' were first described by Heinrich Cornelius Agrippa in *De Occulta Philosophia Libri III* (Three Books of Occult Philosophy), which he finished around 1510 but only published in 1531. Agrippa claimed that the scripts were extremely ancient and, in the case of Celestial, of divine origin, but it is likely that they were created by Agrippa himself, his teacher Johannes Trithemius or some other unidentified sixteenth-century occultist.

Heinrich Cornelius Agrippa (1486–1535) is one of those extraordinary Renaissance polymaths who dabbled in an astounding number of professions. He was successively, and sometimes simultaneously, a theologian, soldier, diplomat, physician, lawyer and occultist, though it is as the latter that he is now remembered. The son of minor German nobility from the town of Nettesheim (in present-day North Rhine-Westphalia), he was sent to the nearby University of Cologne aged thirteen, graduating with a master's degree at sixteen. This does not mean that Agrippa was a child prodigy, because the universities of the day were the equivalent of modern high schools.

His interest in magic was sparked in Cologne and deepened when he studied in Paris, where he is said to have joined a secret society devoted to the study of the occult. In 1508 he took a break from academia, travelling to Spain to become a mercenary fighting for the Holy Roman Emperor Maximilian I. He resumed his professorial career in 1509, lecturing at the University of Dole in Burgundy (now eastern France) but was forced to leave his post because of his unorthodox views about witchcraft and interest in magic and the Kabbalah. In 1510 he studied under Johannes Trithemius, to whom he dedicated his *De Occulta*

Philosophia, which Trithemius advised him never to publish. Continuing his chequered career as a diplomat, theologian, soldier and physician for the next twenty years, Agrippa knew brief periods of imprisonment, but he was always released thanks to his influential connections. In 1531 he published *De Occulta Philosophia*, which was immediately anathematized by the Office of the Holy Inquisition. Despite his conflict with the Catholic Church, he was never seriously persecuted. On two occasions, in 1525 and 1533, he publicly renounced all interest in magic, but this may have been merely a shrewd move on his part to placate his more fanatical Christian opponents.

Heinrich Cornelius Agrippa.

MALACHIM

The origins of the three scripts in *De Occulta Philosophia* are unknown, though their letter names and forms are based on, or derived from, the characters of the Hebrew alphabet. Malachim is the plural of *mal'ach*, the Hebrew word for 'messenger' or 'angel'. We can reject as spurious the claims made by Agrippa that these scripts were used by Moses and the prophets, because they are clearly much later inventions, first appearing in Agrippa's unpublished 1510 manuscript of *De Occulta Philosophia*, which he dedicated to his teacher, Johannes Trithemius. It is possible that Trithemius, one suggested creator of the Theban alphabet, may also have had a hand in Malachim, Passing of the River and Celestial. Some scholars have pointed out that Passing of the River had already appeared in the works of other occultists, published in 1523, 1529 and 1530, but it is likely that they had had sight of Agrippa's 1510 manuscript and merely pre-empted its publication in 1531. Agrippa also made spurious claims about the origins of Celestial, as the divine language of angels, and Passing of the River, which he described as 'figured amongst the stars', suggesting that it was derived from the work of ancient astrologers. The name Passing of the River, rendered in Latin as Transitus Fluvii, is thought to be a reference to the crossing of the Euphrates by the Hebrews returning from their Babylonian exile.

THE MALACHIM ALPHABET

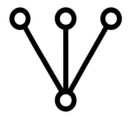

ZAIN

VAU

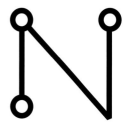

HE

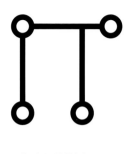

DALETH

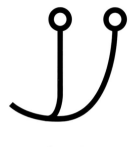

GIMEL

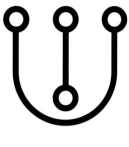

BETH

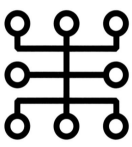

ALEPH

NUN

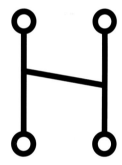

MEM

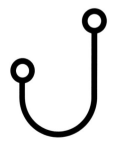

LAMED

CAPH

IOD

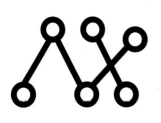

THETH

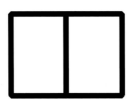

CHETH

RES

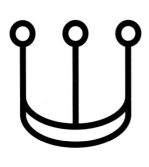

KUFF

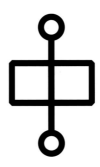

ZADE

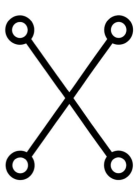

PE

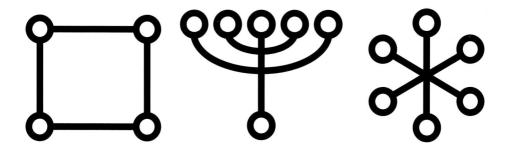

AIN   SATTECH   SAMECH

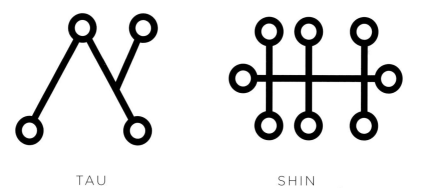

TAU   SHIN

PASSING OF THE RIVER

Heinrich Agrippa's Passing of the River script uses letter names and forms derived from the Hebrew alphabet combined with fanciful letterforms.

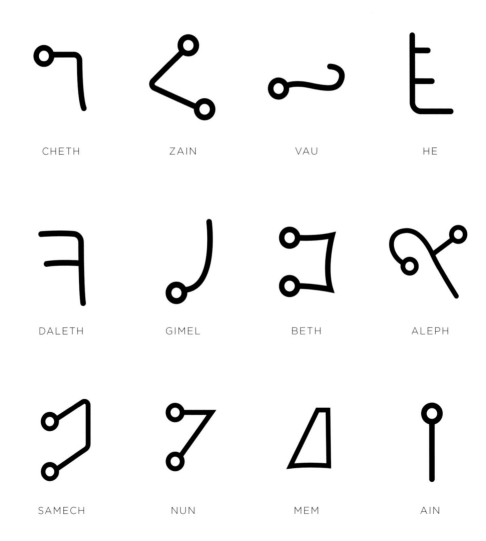

CHETH	ZAIN	VAU	HE
DALETH	GIMEL	BETH	ALEPH
SAMECH	NUN	MEM	AIN

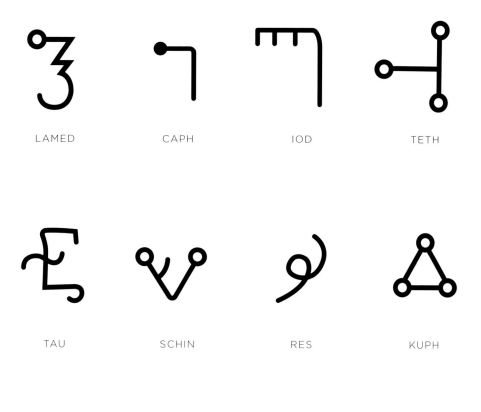

LAMED	CAPH	IOD	TETH

TAU	SCHIN	RES	KUPH

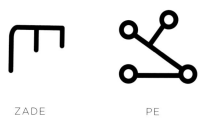

ZADE	PE

CELESTIAL

Heinrich Agrippa's Celestial alphabet works on the same principles as the other two scripts, using invented symbols based on or derived from the Hebrew alphabet. He specifies that Celestial is based on ancient astronomical lore.

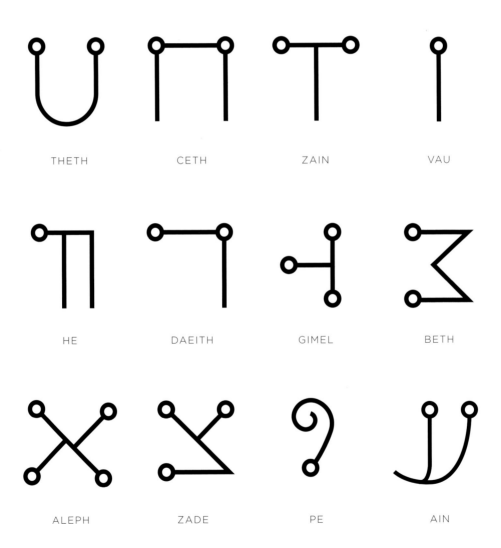

THETH   CETH   ZAIN   VAU

HE   DAEITH   GIMEL   BETH

ALEPH   ZADE   PE   AIN

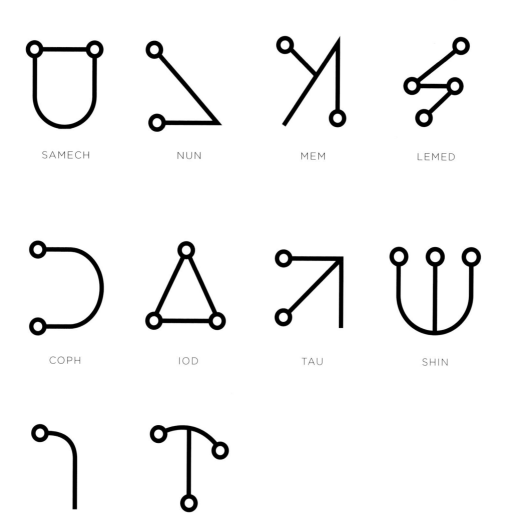

SAMECH

NUN

MEM

LEMED

COPH

IOD

TAU

SHIN

RES

KUFF

ENOCHIAN

Unless you believe that there is such a thing as 'Angelical', the language spoken by the angels, Enochian is a deliberate fraud, but exactly who perpetrated it is the question that we must seek to answer. Enochian first appeared in the works of the sixteenth-century occultist John Dee, but whether he connived in its creation with his collaborator and medium, Edward Kelley, or whether Dee was Kelley's innocent dupe, remains a mystery.

In 1521, the Spanish discovered the secret of turning iron into gold – not through alchemy, but by dispossessing and murdering its Native American owners. Although in the long run the acquisition of so much ill-gotten loot ruined the Spanish Empire, in the sixteenth century it put Spain's rival, England, at a serious disadvantage. King Henry VIII of England made things even worse when he broke away from the Church of Rome. On his death, he bequeathed to his Protestant heirs a bankrupt exchequer, a realm on the brink of civil war, and the ever-present threat of invasion by Catholic Spain backed by the papacy.

Enter one John Dee (1527–c.1609), court astronomer and astrologer, mathematician, alchemist, occultist, patriot and faithful servant of Queen Elizabeth I. Had he been born a century later, Dee would have been a fêted member of the Royal Society, but instead he spent most of his career trying to communicate with angels. In 1582, he met the convicted forger Edward Kelley, or Kelly (1555–c.1598), who persuaded Dee that he was a medium able to communicate with supernatural entities in the angelic language of Enochian. Dee faithfully recorded the missives Kelley transmitted and followed their guidance to the invented letter.

The two men's seven-year association was not a happy one, leading to Dee's financial ruin, Kelley's fathering of a child by Dee's much younger wife, and Kelley's own death when he failed to deliver the formula for the Philosopher's Stone that he had promised to the Holy Roman Emperor Rudolf II. Now to answer the question as to whether Dee was Kelley's accomplice or his dupe: on some level, Dee must have known that Kelley was a fraud, but he had become so invested in his belief in angelic communication that he had no choice but to go along with the deception. Having lost royal patronage on the death of Elizabeth I in 1603, Dee died discredited and impoverished in London, just as England was discovering that trade was a much sounder way of making gold than magic.

John Dee (top), whose lifetime's work was communicating with angels, and (below), Dee's collaborator and medium, Edward Kelley.

Edw: Kelly Prophet or Seer to Dr. Dee.

ENOCHIAN

E
GRAPH

A
UN

F
OR

B
PA

N
DRUX

Q
GER

I/Y
GON

M
TAL

T
GISG

R
DON

O
MED

X
PAL

D
GAL

G/J
GED

C/K
VEH

P
MALS

L
UR

H
NA

S
FAM

U/V
VAN

Z
CEPH

SATOR SQUARE

The Sator or Rotas square consists of five columns and rows of five letters, which spell out the same five words when read vertically or horizontally. Although sator, tenet, opera and rotas are recognizable as Latin nouns or verbs, arepo is not, and has been interpreted as a proper name. However, the words do not constitute a meaningful sentence in Latin or any other language. Regardless of its lack of meaning (or perhaps because of it), the square has been used as a good luck charm to ward off evil since antiquity. It was worn on the person as a talisman or was carved or painted on buildings to protect them and their occupants from fire, thieves and other manmade and natural disasters.

AMULETS

Probably the oldest form of white magic is the wearing of protective talismans or amulets to ward off bad luck and the evil intent of others. Chinese Taoists wore specially minted coins as talismans, which were also offered as 'hell money' to their ancestors to ease their time in the afterlife. Charms can be made in the shape of body parts, such as the Jewish and Arabic *hamsa*, the hand of Fatimah, the Roman phallic *fascinus* and Italian *cornicello*, and the North African *nazar* that wards off the evil eye. Examples of two text-based amulets are the Hebrew *chai*, meaning 'alive', and the Japanese *kanai anzen*, meaning 'safety at home'.

FASCINUS

CORNICELLO

TAOIST TALISMAN COIN

HAMSA

NAZAR

KANAI ANZEN

CHAI

SIGILS

In order to summon the powers of a supernatural entity, a magician needed to know its true name, which differed from its popular name. Hence, the proliferation in medieval and Renaissance grimoires of sigils, from the Latin word *sigillum*, meaning 'small sign' or seal, which represented an angelic or demonic entity's true name by which it could be invoked and controlled. During the premodern period, documents were authenticated with impressions in wax of seals identifying a person or institution; it was natural enough for magicians to apply the same principles to the creation of sigils and seals for the planetary spirits, angels and archangels.

In the popular imagination, medieval and Renaissance magic was largely concerned with the 'black' magic arts of demonology and necromancy, whose symbols we shall explore in the next chapter. Although black magic and demonology did exist, there emerged a parallel tradition of 'white' magic, which sought to invoke and communicate with benign supernatural forces such as angels, archangels and the spirits of the planets. Other powerful sigils created by occultists include the Seal of Solomon, who was the presumed author of several books of magic about the summoning of angels and the control of demons, and the Sigillum Dei, the Sigil of God.

Archangels first make their appearance in the Books of Enoch and Tobit in the Hebrew Bible, the *Tanach*, where they are described as the seven 'watchers' who oversee humanity on God's behalf. The word for 'angel' in Hebrew is *mal'ach*, meaning 'messenger', and the word 'angel' is derived from the Greek *angelos*, also meaning 'messenger'. Archangels also appear in Christianity and Islam, but there is no agreement as to their exact number, powers or names.

Included on the following pages are two sets of archangelic seals created during the Renaissance. The first is identified as coming from the works of Johann Georg Faust (c.1480–1540), the Doctor Faustus made infamous by Christopher Marlowe's play of 1604; and the other is from the seventeenth-century French *Grimoire of Armadel*, which owes its notoriety in occult circles to its having been translated by the British occultist and founder of the Hermetic Order of the Golden Dawn, Samuel Liddell MacGregor Mathers (1854–1918).

In this icon by Theodoros Poulakis (1620–92), Saint Michael the Archangel slays the dragon, as described in the Book of Daniel.

PLANETARY SEALS

In Book II of *De Occulta Philosophia*, Heinrich Cornelius Agrippa gave instructions about how to draw the planetary seals by using the 'table of celestial numbers' corresponding to each heavenly body that identified their 'intelligences' and 'spirits'. He went on to explain how the seals could be used for magical purposes by engraving them on different metals. For example, the seal of Saturn engraved on a sheet of lead could, depending on how it was used, make a man powerful and successful in his petitions to the rich and powerful, or cause him to fall out of favour and fail.

SEAL OF THE SUN

SEAL OF THE MOON

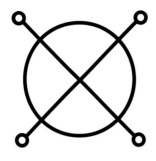

SEAL OF JUPITER

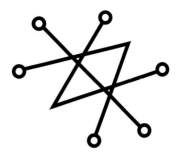

SEAL OF SATURN

SEAL OF VENUS

SEAL OF
MERCURY

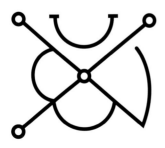

SEAL OF MARS

SIGILS OF THE ARCHANGELS

Compared to the relatively simple designs of Heinrich Cornelius Agrippa's planetary seals, the archangelic sigils of Faust and Armadel are far more complex and include symbols borrowed from astrological lore, including the planets and signs of the zodiac, as well as Greek, Latin and Hebrew characters. The sigils were used as protective talismans and in magical rituals to invoke and summon the power of the archangels to serve the occultist's ends.

ARCHANGELIC SIGILS ACCORDING TO THE GRIMOIRE OF ARMADEL

GABRIEL

MICHAEL

RAPHAEL

SAMUEL

URIEL

ZADKIEL

ARCHANGELIC SIGILS ACCORDING TO JOHANN GEORG FAUST

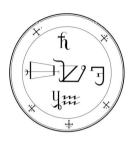

CASSIEL

GABRIEL

MICHAEL

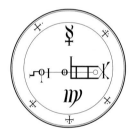

RAPHAEL

SACHIEL

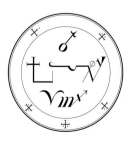

SAMAEL

SIGILLUM DEI

To the modern reader, the idea of an occultist using the name of the Christian God for magical purposes must appear to be a contradiction in terms, because our view of magic places it in direct opposition to religion. To Dee, who, despite his interest in the occult, was a serious scientist and a devout Christian, white magic was a branch of knowledge that he could use for the betterment of humanity. The details of the Sigillum Dei, bearing the name of God and his archangels, had been revealed to him by Edward Kelley, who claimed to have received it from the angels themselves. Thus, Dee had no doubt that he could use the sigil for magical ends without incurring the censure of God.

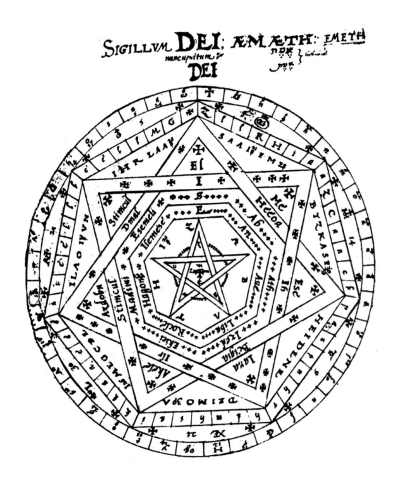

SEAL OF SOLOMON

In Islamic folklore, Allah granted King Solomon the power to control the demonic entities known as *djinn*, from which the word 'genie' is derived. Unlike the friendly Disney caricature of the genie of the lamp, djinn were malevolent entities that were more likely to harm humans than to help them. The legend goes that Solomon's power was channelled through a magic ring, made of iron and brass and inscribed with a six-pointed star, or hexagram, better known to us as the Star of David, the emblem of Judaism and of the State of Israel. Occultists used the seal of Solomon as a talisman to protect themselves from demons and black magic.

CARTOMANCY

Playing cards were introduced to Europe in the late fourteenth century, and immediately engendered the disapproval of the Church – not because of any association with cartomancy (divination with playing or Tarot cards), but because they were associated with sloth, frivolous pleasure and gambling. Fortune-telling with cards emerged much later, in the late eighteenth century, when it brought to prominence new kinds of occultists who were closer to popular entertainers than seekers of forbidden occult knowledge.

With the emergence of cartomancy, we begin to see a redefinition of the relationship between certain occult practices, the Christian churches and wider society. In previous centuries, occultism and magic, be it white or black, had directly challenged Christian teaching with novel theological and cosmological explanations based on ancient learning or alchemical theories. But by the eighteenth century, the churches were facing a far greater challenge from the new rationality spearheaded by the writings of the Enlightenment *philosophes* and scientific discoveries, which equated a belief in revealed scriptural religion with the superstitious belief in the power of magic and of the occult.

Cartomancy did have its serious occult basis, first proposed by Antoine Court de Gébelin (1725–84), a French Protestant pastor and freemason, who was therefore already marginalized in predominantly Catholic pre-revolutionary France. In his multi-volume work *Le Monde primitif* (The Primitive World), Court theorized the existence of an advanced universal pre-classical culture and language. Although he made serious contributions to the study of linguistics, he is remembered today for an essay he wrote about the Tarot, which he described as the distillation of the ancient Egyptian (but quite imaginary) *Book of Thoth*.

Jean-Baptiste Alliette (1738–91), who reversed his name to Etteilla, claimed Court's work as his own, publishing the first book of Tarot divination in 1785, one year after Court's death. However, he made cartomancy more acceptable by giving it the aspect of a harmless parlour-game entertainment. He was the first professional fortune-teller and made his living from private readings and the sale of books on cartomancy. But the woman who established cartomancy and made a fortune in the process was Marie Anne Lenormand (1772–1843), a draper's daughter from Normandy, who claimed, after their deaths, to have advised such luminaries as Robespierre, Napoleon and Josephine, and Tsar Alexander I.

The traditional pattern used in divination with the Tarot. Here only Major Arcana have been used.

THE FOOL.

THE TOWER.

DEATH.

THE HIGH PRIESTESS.

STRENGTH.

JUDGEMENT.

THE MOON.

THE CHARIOT.

THE WORLD.

TAROT MAJOR ARCANA

The Tarot has its origins in Italian decks of playing cards, with the suits represented by the same symbols used in Islamic Egyptian decks: cups, wands (originally polo sticks), swords and coins. The Tarot consists of four suits each comprising ten number cards and four court cards – king, queen, knight and page – and twenty-two trump cards including a fool. The suit cards and the trumps are known respectively as the Minor and Major Arcana when they occur in the divinatory Tarot. The pack shown here was designed by British occultists Arthur Edward Waite (1857-1942) and Pamela Colman Smith (1878-1951). They were influenced by the work of French occultist Eliphas Lévi (1810-75), who claimed that the Tarot existed at the time of Moses and contained 'the knowledge of the *Book of Hermes*'.

THE LOVERS.

THE CHARIOT.

STRENGTH.

THE HERMIT.

WHEEL of FORTUNE

JUSTICE.

THE HANGED MAN.

DEATH.

TEMPERANCE.

TAROT MAJOR ARCANA

FRENCH PLAYING CARDS

Playing cards were invented in ninth-century Tang dynasty China and, like many other Chinese inventions, they slowly made their way westwards along the Silk Road, first to the Islamic world, reaching Egypt in the eleventh century, and from there to Europe, where the use of playing cards for card games is securely attested in the late fourteenth century. Early playing card decks varied in the number of cards and the names of the suits, before they settled to the four suits used in French packs: *cœurs* (hearts), *piques* (spades), *trèfles* (clubs) and *carreaux* (diamonds). We owe cartomancy with playing cards to the work of Marie Anne Lenormand.

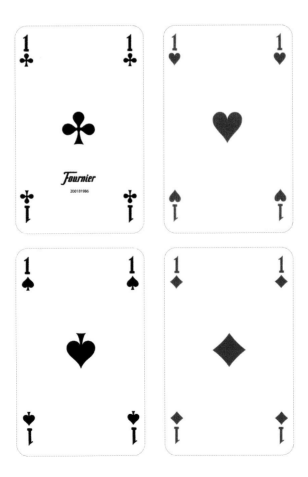

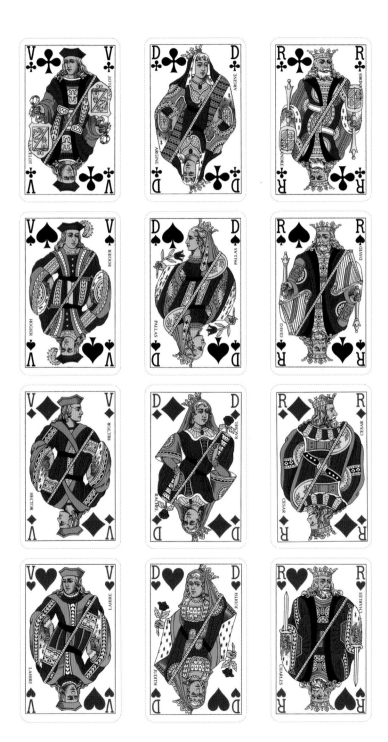

BLACK MAGIC & DEMONOLOGY

The best evidence we have for black magic from the early
modern period is provided by those who were trying to
prove that it existed in order to combat it, and those who
considered that it did not exist and that its practitioners
were either frauds or suffering from mental illness.

Most serious historians accept that the European witch craze that lasted from the mid-fifteenth to the mid-eighteenth centuries, and which may have claimed the lives of up to 100,000 innocent victims, was an example of the madness and delusion of crowds – a kind of moral panic or hysteria caused by the Protestant Reformation and the succeeding conflicts known as the Wars of Religion (1524–1697).

There is no doubt that the vast bulk of the European population during the Renaissance believed in the existence of black magic, witchcraft and demonology, much to the cost of the thousands of poor wretches who were imprisoned, tortured, hanged or burned at the stake as witches. Most of what we know about the practices of witches and demonologists comes from two sources: those who pursued them, and whose power, status and earnings depended on stoking the public hysteria against black magic; and those who argued that witchcraft did not exist and that those who claimed Satanic powers were either conjurers and charlatans or mentally ill.

Leading the witchfinders were the German inquisitor Heinrich Kramer (c.1430–1505) – author of the *Malleus Maleficarum* (The Hammer of the Witches), the source of much of the later folklore of witchcraft – and the self-appointed Witchfinder General of England, Matthew Hopkins (c.1620–47), author of *The Discovery of Witches*. Leading the sceptics were Johann Weyer (1515–88), a Dutch student of Heinrich Cornelius Agrippa and author of *De Praestigiis Daemonum* (The Tricks of Demons,1563), and English parliamentarian Reginald Scot (1538–99), who penned *The Discoverie of Witchcraft* (1584).

Considering how dangerous it was for anyone to claim to be a black magician or demonologist, it is not surprising that the surviving grimoires of medieval and Renaissance black magic are anonymous or attributed to long-dead or fictitious authors such as King Solomon or the mythical mages Abramelin and Honorius of Thebes. In terms of the magical practices and beliefs they describe, they remain within the circumscribed worlds of Renaissance white magical practices, with the same theory of talismans and sigils to invoke the powers of demonic entities, whose designations as 'princes', 'generals' and 'dukes' of Hell corresponded to the hierarchical organization of the choirs of angels and archangels that was modelled on the highly stratified European societies of the time.

Fallen Angel *by Alexandre Cabanel, 1847.*

SET, OR SETH

ancient Egyptian god of the desert and storms.

AHRIMAN, OR ANGRA MAINYU

embodiment of evil in Zoroastrianism.

AHRIMAN & SET

In polytheistic religions that did not have a single omnipresent, omnipotent creator god who represented all that was good, there was no need for a deity who embodied all things evil. For example, in the Greek pantheon, the deity closest to the Christian Satan was Hades, who, though he ruled over the underworld and the lowest hell of Tartarus, where those who had defied and offended the gods were imprisoned and punished, was not himself evil, nor did he try to corrupt humans since everyone, good or bad, ended up in his domain. Likewise, the characterization of the god Set as evil is a misinterpretation of his role in ancient Egyptian religion. It is in dualistic Zoroastrianism that we find the first true embodiment of evil in the demonic figure of Ahriman, whom some scholars believe to have influenced the Christian conception of the devil.

The ancient Egyptian god Set (or Seth) represented the chaos and disorder of the desert and storms. When the Assyrians, Persians and Greeks conquered Egypt, Set was demonized as the god of foreigners. In his incarnation as the god of the wilderness, Set was cast as the enemy of Osiris and his son Horus, who represented the order and civilization of the Nile Valley, but he also had a more positive role in Egyptian religion, as the helper of Amun-Ra, chief of all the gods, who fought the monstrous, world-devouring serpent Apophis.

Zoroastrianism has been described as a dualistic religion, in which the forces of light, represented by Ahura Mazda, and of darkness, represented by Ahriman, also known as Angra Mainyu, are in balance, reminiscent of the Chinese concepts of yin and yang. But in its later iterations, Zoroastrianism became more monotheistic, with Ahriman as the personification of evil who led humans astray, but who would be defeated by Ahura Mazda before the Day of Judgment – an eschatology very reminiscent of later Christian doctrines of good and evil, sin and Last Judgment.

In medieval theology, the all-powerful Christian God of light and goodness needed a dark demonic foil to justify the existence of evil in the world and to explain the doctrine of the Fall, when the serpent tempted Adam and Eve in the Garden of Eden. Mirroring the hierarchical nature of the heavenly host, with its archangels and choirs of angels, the demonic legions, led by princes, dukes and generals, served their emperor, the fallen angel Lucifer, who became evil incarnate as Satan.

PERSONIFICATIONS
OF EVIL

There is no concept of evil incarnate in Judaism, which considers humans as perfectly able to lead themselves astray and disobey God's commandments without the assistance of demons. But Christian theology has always been faced with the problem of explaining how an omnipotent, omnipresent God of love and forgiveness can allow evil to exist in the world. The answer was a foil to the God of love, embodying all that is hateful and bad. But how could such a being exist, since he, too, would be a creation of God? In the account of the Fall, Lucifer, in his pride and arrogance, defies God and rebels to become Satan, lord of Hell.

LUCIFER

The sigil of the fallen angel Lucifer, also known as Morningstar, associated with the planet Venus. He is cast out of heaven and becomes the beast and the father of lies, Satan, the great adversary of Christian and Islamic theology.

SATAN

In the popular imagination, the inverted pentagram is a symbol of black magic and all things Satanic. Satan is associated with the serpent who tempts Adam and Eve, and thus is responsible for the original sin that gives humans free will and condemns them to death. His role becomes that of corrupter-in-chief of the damned, whom he will punish in perpetuity after the Day of Judgment.

THE ANTICHRIST

The Antichrist, identified by the 'Number of the Beast', which, as we have seen, is sometimes given as 666 (see page 146). In his Christian incarnation in the 'End Times', Satan is the Antichrist, the beast – the anti-Messiah who is born into the world of men and brings it to a close in the final climactic battle of Armageddon.

BAPHOMET &
THE TEMPLARS

According to confessions obtained by torture, the Knights Templar worshipped an idol made in the shape of a half-man, half-goat Satanic figure called Baphomet. Although they recanted their confessions, the accused were eventually burned at the stake as Satanists and heretics; but what was the real reason behind their arrest and prosecution, and was there any truth in accusations of the idolatrous worship of Baphomet?

Twenty years after the conquest of Jerusalem in 1099, and the establishment of the crusader kingdoms of Outremer, the Holy Land remained so dangerous and bandit-infested that a French knight named Hugues de Payens (1070–1136) petitioned the king of Jerusalem to allow him to establish an order of Christian knights to protect pilgrims and the holy sites. The king agreed and headquartered the Poor Fellow-Soldiers of Christ and of the Temple of Solomon (or Templars) in the Islamic Dome of the Rock and Al-Aqsa Mosque on Jerusalem's Temple Mount, which the knights believed to be the remains of King Solomon's Temple.

The crusader states endured until 1192, when the Christians were expelled by Arab armies commanded by Saladin. The Templars withdrew to the island of Cyprus. Having lost their original purpose, they amassed considerable wealth as international traders and bankers, establishing what has been described as the world's first multinational corporation, lending money to the crowned heads of Europe, including King Philip IV 'the Fair' of France. In 1307, Philip invited Templar Grand Master Jacques de Molay, ostensibly to discuss the financing of a new crusade. In reality, the king, who was perennially short of cash and heavily in debt, had decided on a novel solution to his financial woes: he

would seize the wealth of the Templars. However, in order to prove his case against an ancient and respected order of celibate Christian knights, he would have to demonstrate that they were guilty of the most heinous crimes against God and the Church. Under torture, the knights admitted to sorcery, sodomitic initiation rituals and the idolatrous worship of Baphomet.

Baphomet was the name given by medieval Christians to what they thought was an Islamic idol, as they mistakenly believed Islam to be a polytheistic pagan religion. The Near Eastern origins of the order probably gave Philip and his advisers the idea of accusing them of idolatry, as well as certain initiatory practices of the Templars that may have featured the use of some kind of 'idol'.

Two conjectural reconstructions of Baphomet, the idol alleged to have been worshipped by the Knights Templar and used during their blasphemous initiation rituals. If such an idol ever existed and was not a creation of the vivid imagination of Philip's inquisitors, it must have been destroyed long before these images were created in the nineteenth and twentieth centuries. The myth of the Templars and their presumed ownership of the Ark of the Covenant and the Holy Grail has fuelled a very lucrative franchise of pseudohistorical books and TV shows.

SIGIL WITH THE PENTANGLE
OF BAPHOMET

THE 'SABBATICAL GOAT' IN THE
GUISE OF BAPHOMET

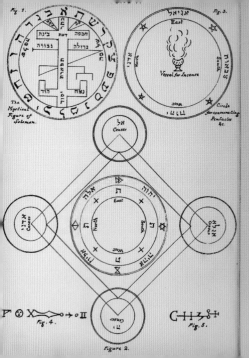

THE

KEY OF SOLOMON THE KING

(*CLAVICULA SALOMONIS*)

Now first Translated and Edited from Ancient MSS. in the
British Museum

BY

S. LIDDELL MACGREGOR MATHERS

Author of "The Kabbalah Unveiled," "The Tarot," &c.

WITH PLATES

LONDON
GEORGE REDWAY
YORK STREET COVENT GARDEN
1889

GRIMOIRES

The entire tradition of Western demonology rests on a handful of grimoires – a French word derived from *grammaires* (grammars), originally referring to any book written in Latin. Most extant versions of black magic grimoires can be securely dated to the eighteenth and nineteenth centuries, but they are claimed to date back to the medieval and early modern periods or even to antiquity. Several are known to us only because they were used as illustrations of the conjuring tricks of fraudulent occultists or of the ramblings of the mentally ill. The most famous owe their notoriety to the fact that they were translated, edited and illustrated by nineteenth- and twentieth-century occultists.

In a preliterate society, a handwritten parchment book covered in arcane drawings could be a copy of an ancient text on agronomy or Euclidian geometry, or a grimoire full of incantations to conjure and control demons. There is no doubt that for black magicians, demonologists and necromancers seeking to impress potential clients, the ownership of ancient manuscripts and grimoires was a potent marketing tool, on a par with the fake degrees and doctorates hanging on the walls of today's snake oil salesmen.

Of course, black magic grimoires did exist. They typically contained instructions on how to use supernatural forces to gain riches and the favour of powerful men and to control others, usually by summoning and invoking demonic entities. They were written in ancient languages or cyphers to prevent the uninitiated from understanding their magical secrets.

The two best known grimoires are the *Key of Solomon* (*Clavicula Salomonis*) and the *Lesser Key of Solomon* (also known as *Lemegeton* or *Ars Goetia*) – both attributed to the long-dead King Solomon, because any living person claiming authorship would have immediately found himself arraigned in front of the courts of the Holy Office of the Inquisition and liable to imprisonment, torture and execution. According to nineteenth- and twentieth-century occultists, such as Eliphas Lévi, Aleister Crowley and Samuel Liddell MacGregor Mathers, who sought to maximize the sales of their translations, the most dangerous grimoire of the Solomonic tradition was *Le Grand Grimoire*, some of whose 'terrifying' illustrations are reproduced on pages 216–19. Other works of black magic include *Le Grimoire du Pape Honorius*, which is most likely an anti-Catholic Protestant hoax, attributed to a pious thirteenth-century pope known for his theological writings, and the amusing *Les Douze Anneaux* (The Twelve Rings), which instructs the male reader how to create charms that will allow him to bed maidens and increase the milk yield of his cattle.

Nineteenth-century edition of The Key of Solomon the King, translated by S. Liddell MacGregor Mathers, founder of the Hermetic order of the Golden Dawn.

LES DOUZE ANNEAUX

The short French-language grimoire *Les Douze Anneaux* (The Twelve Rings) presents twelve talismans that are to be carved onto rings to achieve a range of magical effects ranging from mundane success in hunting and fishing, to curing various diseases, to the more fantastical, such as invisibility. The self-interested could learn how to get a maiden into bed, to defeat one's enemies and to gain the favour of powerful men. 'Gabriach' is the Star of David, also known as the Seal of Solomon, that was believed to protect against demons. The endings in T and CH suggest that the author was trying to establish a link to Hebrew, but 'Dalet' doesn't resemble the Hebrew letter D, and 'Astarot' is unlike the symbol for the demon Astaroth in the *Ars Goetia*. *Les Douze Anneaux* was the work of someone with enough knowledge of magical alphabets, sigils and Hebrew letters to create a pastiche of their own.

DALET
For success in a stag hunt.

ASTAROT
To get a familiar spirit.

ASMALIOR
To 'know' a woman or maiden.

TONUCHO
To become invisible.

GABRIOT
For having a horse that never tires.

BALSAMIACH
To cure any illness and heal all wounds.

GABRIACH
To protect from all evil spirits.

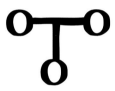

DOLOFECH
To heal problems of vision.

BALBUCH
To ensure a good catch of fish.

JAMPELUCH
To ensure a good haul of wild birds.

TOPINOCH
To vanquish one's enemies.

ILLUSABIO
To earn the favour of the powerful.

LE GRAND GRIMOIRE

Known mainly from eighteenth-century copies, *Le Grand Grimoire* is thought to date
to the early sixteenth century. This anonymous French text of black magic describes the
leading demons of hell, whose titles are clearly modelled on an earthly hierarchy, and
outlines the techniques used to summon and control them. The nineteenth-century
French occultist Eliphas Lévi is said to have identified it as one of the leading magical
texts. It was translated into English by the British occultist Arthur Edward Waite, one
of the designers of the Rider–Waite Tarot pack. The text gives titles to various demons,
creating an imaginary hierarchy of Hell. Lucifer is identified as the 'emperor' of Hell and
represented with a jester's hat as the 'Prince of Fools', as well as the more conventional
horned and winged demon with a pitchfork. The other demons are associated with other
figures of fun, insects and animals, as well as motifs taken from Greco-Roman pagan art,
including the head of a satyr (Astaroth) and a sphinx (Lucifuge).

LUCIFER, EMPEROR

BEELZEBUB, PRINCE

ASTAROTH, GRAND DUKE

LUCIFUGE, PRIME MINISTER

SATANACHIA, GREAT GENERAL

FLEURETY, LIEUTENANT GENERAL

NEBIROS, FIELD MARSHAL

ARS GOETIA
DEMONIC SIGILS

The *Ars Goetia* (the *Lemegeton* or *Lesser Key of Solomon*) is known in two versions, one listing sixty-nine demons, found in Johann Weyer's *Pseudomonarchia Daemonum* (The False Monarchy of Demons), and the other listing seventy-two demons, in Reginald Scot's *Discoverie of Witchcraft*, two books that denied the existence of black magic and demonology, and attempted to show that black magicians were either frauds or, if sincere in their beliefs, suffering from mental illness. The *Ars Goetia* owes its fame in occult circles to its translation by Samuel Liddell MacGregor Mathers with an introduction and illustrations by Aleister Crowley (1875–1947), the notorious British occultist.

BAEL

AGARES

VASSAGO

GAMIGIN

MARBAS

VALEFAR

BERITH

ASTAROTH

FORNEUS

BELETH

LERAJE

ELIGOS

AAMON

BARBATOS

PAIMON

BUER

GUSION

SITRI

ARS GOETIA DEMONIC SIGILS

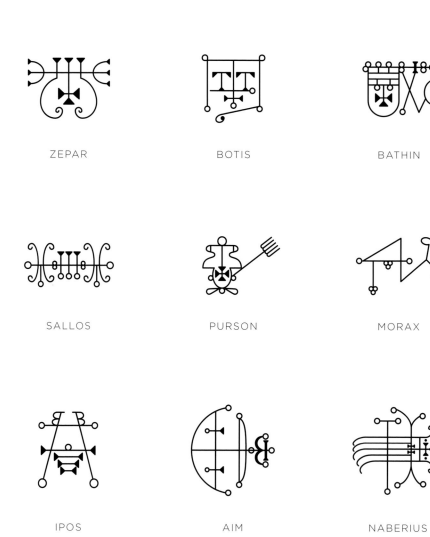

ZEPAR

BOTIS

BATHIN

SALLOS

PURSON

MORAX

IPOS

AIM

NABERIUS

GLASYA-LABOLAS

BUNE

RONOVE

FORAS

ASMODEUS

GAAP

FURFUR

MARCHOSIAS

STOLAS

PHENEX

HALPHAS

MALPHAS

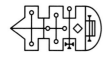

RAUM

FOCALOR

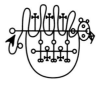

VEPAR

SABNOCK

SHAX

VINE

BIFRONS

VUAL

HAAGENTI

CROCELL

FURCAS

BALAM

ALLOCER

CAIM

MURMUR

OROBAS

GREMORY

OSE

AMY

ORIAS

VAPULA

ZAGAN

VALAC

ANDRAS

HAURES

ANDREALPHUS

KIRMARIS

AMDUSIAS

BELIAL

DECARABIA

SEERE

DANTALION

ANDROMALIUS

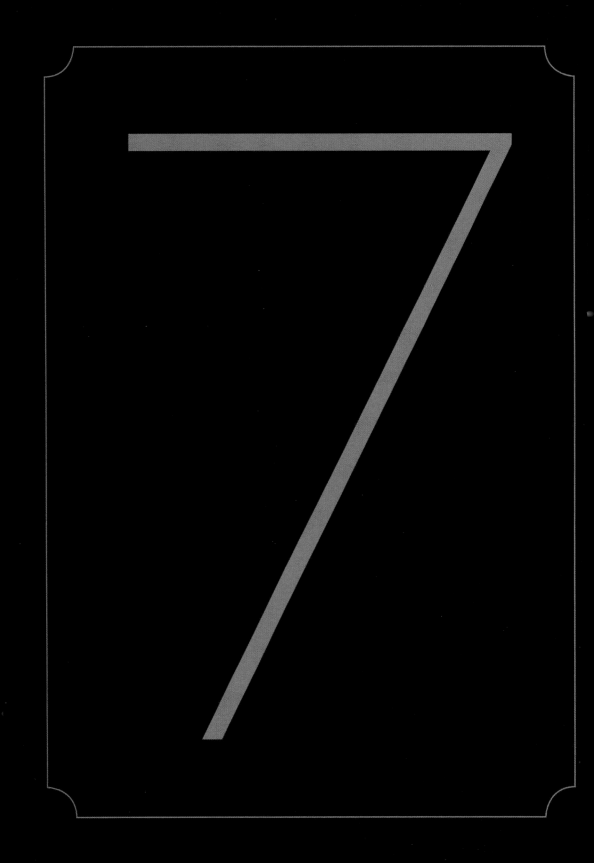

WESTERN ESOTERIC TRADITION

There is no single Western occult tradition but a series
of disparate groups and movements. Together, these
constitute the several phases of occultism that have
emerged in response to the major intellectual, political
and religious shifts since the Renaissance. They seem
more closely related than they really are, because of their
shared use of the same repertoire of occult symbols.

It is possible to identify four major phases of the Western occult tradition since the Renaissance, beginning with the introduction of the Kabbalah, which elevated folk magic to a serious intellectual pursuit. There was a break with Renaissance occultism during the Age of Enlightenment, with the emergence of secret societies with both occult and radical social and political agendas. In the late nineteenth century, the occult was reconfigured as a rejection of established religion, Victorian morality and scientific materialism. This in turn fed into the counterculture of the 1960s, whose occult expressions were the New Age movements that stressed the importance of environmental concerns and offered individuals new paths to spiritual growth and renewal.

With the introduction of Neo-Platonic philosophy and the Kabbalah during the Renaissance, humanist scholars attempted what amounted to an 'occult reformation' of the Catholic Church, which was mired in corrupt practices such as the sale of indulgences, and had become the target of reformers because of its belief in the power of relics. The Protestant Reformation put paid to these attempts, and both denominations turned against occultism – the Protestants because it smacked of Catholic 'superstition', and the Catholics because it promoted an unorthodox theology with strong Jewish overtones.

Persecution forced occultists underground, and they coalesced into private associations that would be transformed into the Enlightenment secret societies, which were the shared homes of occultists and social visionaries. The Kabbalah retained its central role, giving a sense of continuity, but its interpretation shifted with the changing intellectual and religious landscape that was about to be transformed once more by the American and French revolutions.

The final two phases of the occult, from the late nineteenth century until the present day, are born of the same rejection of materialism, conventional morality and science on the one hand, and of established Christian teaching on the other. Organizations such as the Theosophical Society and the Hermetic Order of the Golden Dawn looked back to Renaissance and Enlightenment occultism, as well as to the esoteric traditions of South and East Asia. New Age occult movements were the heirs of *fin-de-siècle* anti-Christian and anti-materialist occultism, which found expression in the varied symbolic traditions of Wicca, Satanism, and Celtic, Germanic–Norse and Slavic Neo-Paganism.

The All-Seeing Eye, or Eye of God in the Clementine Gallery, Vatican Museums.

KABBALAH, CABALA, QABALAH

There are at least three different traditions referred to as the *Kabbalah, Cabala* and *Qabalah*. The first refers to the esoteric Jewish Kabbalah that had a magical counterpart in the practical Kabbalah; the second refers to the Christian Cabala of the European Renaissance; and the third refers to the Hermetic Qabalah of the secret societies that first emerged in Europe in the late seventeenth century.

Reconstructing the history and relationships of the disparate Kabbalistic traditions, which each had numerous schools and interpretations, is made more complicated by the claims of antiquity made by their respective adherents. The Jewish Kabbalah, it was claimed, went back to Adam and Eve and the Garden of Eden, though it is now accepted by scholars to date from the twelfth century; it reached Christian Europe via Muslim Spain and Sicily along with Islamic translations of the Hermetic Corpus. As the Christian Cabala, once attributed to Moses, it was adapted as a vehicle for Christian salvation; as the Hermetic Qabalah, it was associated with the magical Greco-Egyptian teachings of Hermes Trismegistus, to serve occult and alchemical purposes.

The Italian humanist Giovanni Pico della Mirandola (1463–94), who was a protégé of the Medici in Florence, is credited as the formulator of the Christian Cabala. His work was taken forward by other Renaissance scholars, including the Jesuit friar, linguist and Egyptologist Athanasius Kircher (1602–80). When Heinrich Cornelius Agrippa (1486–1535) lectured on the Qabalah at the University of Dole in France, he was accused of being a 'Judaizing heretic' and had to leave his post. The Hermetic Qabalah became an integral part of the Enlightenment

occult as well as the teachings of several nineteenth- and early twentieth-century occultists, including Samuel Liddell MacGregor Mathers, one of the founders of the Hermetic Order of the Golden Dawn, and his one-time disciple Aleister Crowley, who created the Thelema religion.

The main symbol associated with the Kabbalah is the *sefirot*, also known as the Tree of Life, which is a diagrammatic representation of the ten emanations or attributes of God, through which he makes himself manifest in the world. The sefirot can also represent ten degrees on a spiritual path towards union with God, and in later ceremonial occultism, different grades of initiation in secret societies.

Christian interpretation of the Cabala, from Athanasius Kircher's Oedipus Aegyptiacus (1652–54).

SEFIROT

Here are four different renderings of the sefirot, or Tree of Life, whose ten linked nodes represent the attributes, or emanations, of God made manifest in the world, and the stages of the Kabbalistic spiritual and occult paths towards union with the divine. While retaining the basic structure of the sefirot, Cabala and Qabalah reinterpreted its nodes and links according to Christian or occult notions. Its symbolism was later associated with the degrees or grades initiates had to pass through in order to progress within Enlightenment secret societies and nineteenth- and twentieth-century magical orders.

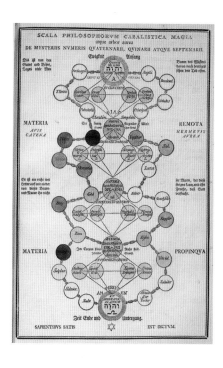

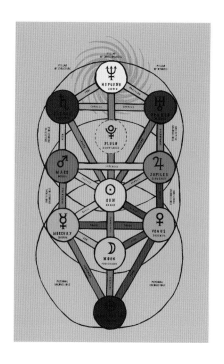

SCALA PHILOSOPHORVM
CABALISTICA MAGIA

COLOURED SEFIROTIC
TREE ILLUSTRATION

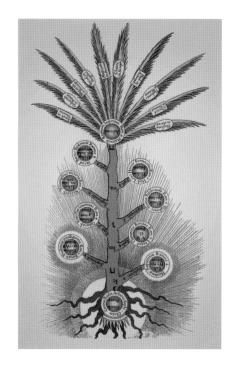

SEFIROTIC TREE AND THE
DIVINE ATTRIBUTES

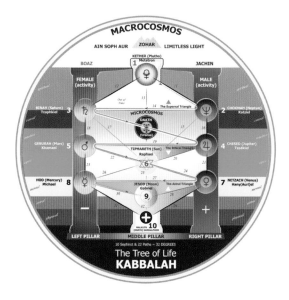

TREE OF LIFE WITH
PILLARS

SECRET SOCIETIES

The secret societies of the Age of Enlightenment began with a seventeenth-century hoax about the existence of a secret order of Rosicrucian sages working to reform humanity. This prompted the creation of real secret societies dedicated to the advancement of humanity, following Enlightenment principles and using the language and symbolism of the occult. The societies that emerged in the eighteenth century included Rosicrucianism, Martinism and, the most famous, Freemasonry, whose first official lodge opened in London in 1717. These groups were home to Christian mystics and occultists as well as scientists, social visionaries and political radicals, among them Sir Isaac Newton (1643–1727), Benjamin Franklin (1706–90) and George Washington (1732–99), who joined the Freemasons to promote and pursue the social, political and scientific aims of the Enlightenment.

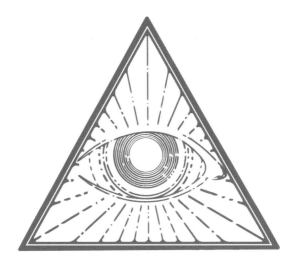

FREEMASONRY
ALL-SEEING EYE

The symbol first appeared in a work of American
Mason Thomas Smith Webb in 1797. It symbolizes
the omnipresence and omnipotence of the deity as
the supreme architect of the universe. It is also found
on the Great Seal of the United States.

FREEMASONRY
SQUARE AND COMPASSES

The square and compasses are the traditional tools of
the medieval masons who built the cathedrals. They have
both literal and metaphorical meanings and are used
in Masonic rituals and initiations. The letter G refers to
either 'God' or 'Geometry'.

GRAND YORK RITE

The symbol is made using the St Anthony's Cross, based on the Greek letter Tau.

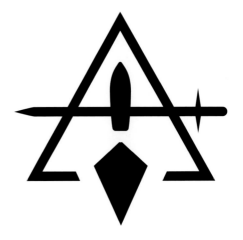

GRAND YORK RITE

The symbol consists of a mason's trowel and a knight's sword. The sword is associated with the Knights Templar.

GRAND YORK RITE

The symbol combines the crown of salvation with a knight's sword.

SCOTTISH RITE

The double-headed eagle was associated
with the Byzantine and Russian monarchies.
Here it is combined with the crown
and sword.

SCOTTISH RITE

An eagle, head lowered and wings
outstretched, associated with the rose cross,
crown and square and compasses.

SHRINERS

Originally known as the Ancient Arabic Order of the Nobles
of the Mystic Shrine, which explains the Egyptian and Near
Eastern symbolism of their emblem.

ROSICRUCIANISM

The surname of the mythical founder of Rosicrucianism, Christian Rosenkreuz, is German for 'rose cross'. The pairing of ornate Christian crosses with roses, symbols of sensuality, passion and sex, was a provocation to the austere German Lutheran and Calvinist churches that rejected the luxury of Catholic iconography.

ROSE CROSS

ANKH ROSE CROSS

MARTINISM

SEAL OF THE ORDER OF THE ROSE CROSS

Although Christian, the Martinist orders use Jewish symbols, such as the Star of David, in their emblems.

SEAL OF THE ORDER OF THE GREAT PRIORY

Here the Star of David is combined with a heraldic lion rampant.

TETRAGRAMMATON

The name of God in Hebrew transliterated in the four letters YHWH (Jehovah) set within a heart.

MARTINIST HEART

The heart motif is combined with the Jewish Star of David.

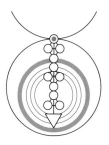

UNIVERSAL TABLE

A diagrammatic version of the sefirot, the Kabbalistic Tree of Life.

OCCULT ORDERS

The occult societies and orders that emerged at the end of the nineteenth century reflected an intellectual atmosphere that questioned the direction society was taking as it became more urban and industrialized. They rejected the period's materialistic and scientific world view, seeking a more spiritual mode of existence that looked back to the Western occult tradition and to the philosophies and spiritual disciplines of South and East Asia. Both the Theosophical Society and the Hermetic Order of the Golden Dawn, who shared members, symbols and beliefs, promoted the existence of 'secret masters' or 'secret chiefs' who were guiding humanity towards an era of spiritual renewal. However sincere some of their adepts may have been, there were others, like Aleister Crowley, who used the occult as a cloak for their own self-aggrandizement and to indulge in an alternative lifestyle that included abusive 'sex magick' and drug use, which earned Crowley the tabloid sobriquet of 'the world's wickedest man'.

THEOSOPHY

The main symbol of Theosophy incorporates the Hindu shatkona and the Egyptian Ankh enclosed in an ouroboros (serpent) topped with a Hindu swastika and the Sanskrit 'Om', meaning 'god'.

THEOSOPHY

The T stands for *theos*, meaning 'god', and the S for *sofia*, meaning 'wisdom'; the choice of the snake is a symbolic rejection of the Christian interpretation of the Fall of Adam and Eve.

THEOSOPHY SRI YANTRA

Theosophy borrowed heavily from Hindu iconography and beliefs as
evidenced by their use of Sri Yantra, a mantra used in Tantric Hinduism
for meditation and magical rituals. The interlocking triangles represent
Siva and Shakti, the male and female principles.

ARGENTIUM ASTRUM ORDER

The seal of the Fraternal Order of the Silver Star consists of
a seven-pointed star with a letter on each point spelling out
the word 'Babalon', a Goddess in the Thelema religion based
on the Whore of Babylon from the Book of Revelation.

HERMETIC ORDER OF THE GOLDEN DAWN

The Golden Dawn's rose cross with the symbols for the tria prima
and the pentagram of the five classical elements around a central
inset rose cross.

HERMETIC ORDER OF THE GOLDEN DAWN

The figure of the crucified Christ within a Star of David,
with archangels and astrological symbols.

HERMETIC ORDER OF THE GOLDEN DAWN

Another version of the Golden Dawn's rose cross.

HERMETIC ORDER OF THE GOLDEN DAWN

The Golden Dawn's version of John Dee's Sigillum Dei, the sigil of God.

HERMETIC ORDER OF
THE GOLDEN DAWN
Another version of the Golden Dawn's rose
cross with Hebrew letters.

HERMETIC ORDER OF
THE GOLDEN DAWN

Symbol of the Golden Dawn consisting of the upward-facing
triangle of Fire and the Christian cross.

HERMETIC ORDER OF
THE GOLDEN DAWN
Platonic solid with astrological symbols.

HERMETIC ORDER OF THE
GOLDEN DAWN
Platonic solid with the rose cross
and ouroboros snakes.

ORDO TEMPLI ORIENTIS

The Ordo Templi Orientis (Order of Oriental Templars) was initially associated with European Freemasonry but it later became associated with the religion Thelema. Shown here are: (top), the emblem of the order that consists of a Wadjet (Eye of Horus), Dove of Peace and Holy Grail containing a rose cross; (below), a chalice, or Holy Grail, with a sword and sceptre.

THELEMA

In Thelema, the six-pointed star is equated with the Egyptian Ankh (key of life) and the Rosicrucian rose cross. The flower at the centre represents the pentacle of the five elements.

THE NEW AGE

It was the postwar reconstruction boom that set off the explosion of youth counterculture in the 1960s. New Age occultism was a rejection of what had gone before, in terms of religious beliefs, morality, politics, and the doctrines of free-market capitalism. Occultism stressed the realization of an individual's potential through the pursuit of magical and spiritual techniques, while advocating new ways of living that would ultimately eliminate hierarchical patriarchy and solve the pollution crisis that was the focus of the ecological movement at that time. New Age occultism looked back to the pagan European past – Neo-Druidism, Celtic and Germanic Norse Neo-Paganism and Slavic Neo-Paganism (Rodnovery, which literally means 'native faith') – and, further back, to Renaissance black magic and demonology. The latter inspired the Church of Satan, founded by Anton LaVey (1930–97), and the breakaway Temple of Set, founded by former Satanist Michael Aquino (b. 1946); while pre-Renaissance folk magic was the inspiration for Wicca, founded by British civil servant Gerald Gardner (1884–1964).

 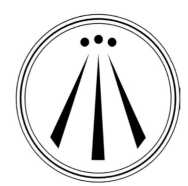

NEO-DRUIDIC AWEN

Two versions of the Neo-Druidic Awen, which means 'inspiration' in the ancient Celtic languages of Welsh, Cornish and Breton. The exact meaning of the symbol varies but can be seen to relate to several important pagan triads, including earth, sea and air; love, wisdom and truth; or body, mind and spirit, as well as representing the rays of the Sun at the 'Triad of Sunrises' through the solar year.

NEO-PAGANISM

Neo-Paganism describes a group of new religions that claim descent from the polytheistic religions of pre-Christian Europe, which themselves had their origins in the religions of the original Indo-European settlers of India, the Middle East and Europe. Germanic, Slavic (Rodnovery), Celtic, Norse and Greco-Roman Neo-Pagans share pantheons of divinities with similar attributes and styles of worship. Typically, these include the notion of sacrificial offerings to the gods, purification and initiation rituals and festivals timed to the major astronomical events of the year: the solstices and equinoxes (see the Wheel of the Seasons, pages 48–9).

NEO-PAGAN WHEEL OF THE YEAR

The spokes mark the main festivals of the solar year.

RODNOVERY: BELOBOG

God of light.

RODNOVERY: CHERNOBOG

God of darkness.

RODNOVERY: DAZHDBOG

Solar deity and cult hero.

RODNOVERY: VELES

God of earth, waters and the underworld.

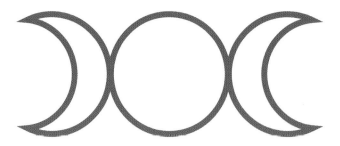

MOTHER GODDESS

The Wicca sign for the Mother Goddess symbolizes two
significant triads: the waxing, full and waning Moon and the
feminine triad of the mother, maiden and crone.

HORNED GOD

The Wicca horned god shares his symbol
with the astrological sign Taurus and ancient
pictographic signs for cattle or bulls.

WITCH SIGN

The Wicca witch sign was scratched into
doorposts to indicate that the homeowner
was sympathetic to witches during times
of persecution.

BLESSINGS

The symbol representing Wicca blessings
is a crescent Moon for the Moon Goddess
and three teardrops signifying the blessings
and the three aspects of maid, mother
and crone.

WITCHES' KNOT

Wicca borrowed this symbol from ancient
pagan and Celtic knot patterns.
It symbolizes the power of the four
elements of air, water, earth and fire.

SPIRITUALITY

Right- and left-handed spirals are two of the most ancient symbols known
to humanity, which first occur in prehistoric cave art. Their original meaning
is unknown but in Wicca the left-handed spiral represents Wicca spirituality
and the right-handed spiral, transmigration and rebirth.

REBIRTH

CHURCH OF SATAN

The emblem of the Church of Satan uses the inverted
pentacle with the head of Baphomet shown within the star.

PENTAGRAM

The classic sign associated with Satanism is the inverted pentagram,
not to be confused with the pentacle, which is a five-pointed star
within a circle. Both pentagram and pentacle, right-side up and
inverted, have been used in all occult traditions.

SIGN OF LEVIATHAN

The sign of the Leviathan consists of a cross of Lorraine over
an infinity symbol, which is favoured by Satanists for ritual use
and protective talismans and tattoos.

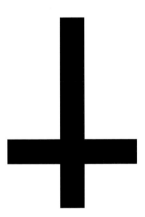

INVERTED CROSS

The inverted cross, which has been adopted by Satanists, has
its origins in the Christian cross of St Peter. When St Peter was
crucified in Rome, he asked to be crucified upside down to
differentiate his martyrdom from the crucifixion of Jesus.

INDEX

A

Adinkra 104-7
aether 36-7, 155
Agrippa, Heinrich Cornelius 164, 166, 170-9, 188, 204, 230
Ahriman (Angra Mainyu) 206-7
air 18, 36-8, 68, 132, 155, 251
alchemy 22, 36, 123-31, 180
All-Seeing Eye 234
amulets 185
angels 165, 172, 180-3, 186-7, 190-2, 204-5, 207-8, 242
Angkor Wat 152-3
Ankh 88, 238, 240, 247
Antichrist 209
Aquarius 17, 18, 22, 24, 37
Argentium Astrum 241
Aries (Ares) 10, 13, 15, 18, 22, 24, 36-7
Ark of the Covenant 211
Armadel 186, 190
Armageddon 209
Ars Goetia 213, 214, 220-5
astrology 9-21, 22-9, 80, 84-5, 94, 130, 135, 164, 180, 242, 245
astronomy 14, 30-1, 84-5, 180
Awen 248
Ayurveda 127

B

Babylonians 14, 17, 79, 80-1, 83, 84, 144
bagua 38, 40-1
Baphomet 210-11, 252
Beltane 48-9
bodhi tree 46-7
buffalo 52-4
bull 15, 90, 250

C

Cabala 230-3
Cancer 15, 18, 22, 24, 36-7
Capricorn 17, 18, 22, 24, 37
cardinal points 20, 52-5, 116-19, 153, 156, 161
Carnac 153
cartomancy 163, 164, 194-201
Celestial 170, 178-9
Celtic symbols 98-9, 228

chakras 66-9
China 26-9, 108-11, 126-7, 145, 160-1, 185, 199
Church of Satan 248, 252-3
copper 134-5
cross 98-9, 236-8, 242-5, 253
Crowley, Aleister 213, 220, 230, 240
cuneiform 79-85, 145

D

death 20, 65, 66, 71, 74, 117, 150, 153, 156
decans 22
Dee, John 164, 180-1, 192, 243
demonology 164, 186, 203-25, 248
demotic 86
divination stones 56-61
dog 26-7, 29, 43, 59, 118
Douze Anneaux, Les 213, 214-15

E

eagle 13, 52-4, 118, 237
earth 18, 36-8, 68, 132, 155, 251
Earth Mother 61, 250
Earth Sisters 57, 60
Egyptians 86-9, 145
elements
  classical 18, 26, 36-7, 128, 132, 141, 155, 242, 247, 251
  mundane 136-7
  tria prima 133, 242
enata 64-5
Enochian 180-3
Eye of God 229
Eye of Horus 89, 246

F

Faust, Johann Georg 186, 190, 191
feng shui 40, 160-1
fire 18, 36-8, 68, 132, 155, 244, 251
foetus 64
Freemasonry 234-7, 246

G

galdrastafur 102-3
gematria 144, 146-7
Gemini 15, 18, 22, 24, 37

geomancy 26, 38, 40, 42, 160-1
geometry 152-5, 235
goat 17, 24, 26-7, 29, 206-7, 210-11, 252
gold 134-5, 140
Greek alphabet 94-8, 144, 147, 172
grimoires 186, 190, 212-25

H

Haab' 30-1
Hebrew 144, 146-7, 172, 176, 178, 185, 186, 190, 214, 239, 242, 244-5
Hermes Trismegistus 125, 128, 130, 230
Hermetic Order of the Golden Dawn 228, 230, 240, 242-5
Hermetica 128
Hermeticism 18
hexagrams 40
hieroglyphs 86-9
Holy Grail 211, 246
Honorius 166-9, 204
horse 17, 26-7, 29, 101, 102, 108-11
Horus 22, 207, 246
humours 18, 36-7

I

I Ching 38, 40, 108-11
Icelandic staves 102-3
ideograms 79-85, 102-3, 108, 116-19
Imbolc 48-9
iron 134-5
isopsephy 144, 146-7

J

Jupiter 12-13, 135, 189

K

Kabbala 124, 130-1, 164, 170, 228, 230-3, 239
Kelley, Edward 180, 192
Key of Solomon 212-13
Kircher, Athanasius 230-1
Knights Templar 210-11, 236, 246
knots 98-9, 251

L

Lammas 48-9
lead 134-5
Lemegeton 213, 220-5

Leo 16, 18, 22, 24, 36–7
Lesser Key of Solomon 213, 220-5
Libra 16, 18, 22, 24, 37
Litha 48–9
logograms 86
Lucifer 207, 208, 216
luopan 160

M
Mabon 48–9
Magnum Opus 140–1
Malachim 170, 172–5
mandala 156–7
mantra 66–9
Mars 12–13, 135, 189
Martinism 234, 239
Mathers, SLM 186, 213, 220
Maya 30–1, 116–19
medicine wheel 52–5
Mercury 10, 12–13, 135, 189
mercury (quicksilver) 133, 134–5
monkey 26–7, 29, 118
Moon 10, 12–13, 24, 39, 135, 188, 250

N
nadis 66–7, 69
necromancy 164, 186, 213
Neo-Paganism 49, 228, 248–53
Neo-Platonism 228
Neptune 12–13
New Age movement 228, 248–53
Number of the Beast 146, 209, 220
numerology 94, 144–51, 154

O
Ogham tree alphabet 50–1
onomancy 146
oracle bones 108–11
Ostara 48–9

P
Paracelsus 133, 166
Passing of the River 170, 176–7
pentacle 247, 252
pentagram 209, 242, 252
pentangle 211
Phaistos pictograms 90–3
Philosopher's Stone 128, 136, 138, 140–1, 180

phoenix 42, 44, 111
pictograms 78, 80, 82, 86–93, 102, 142, 144, 250
Pisces 17, 18, 22, 24, 36–7
planetary seals 188
Platonic solids 155, 245
prana 66
Pythagoreanism 94, 144, 146, 148, 154

Q
Qabalah 230–3
qi 38–9, 126

R
Rodnovery 249
Rongorongo 112–15
rose cross 237, 238, 242–5, 247
Rosicrucianism 234, 238, 247
runes 100–1, 102

S
Sagittarius 17, 18, 22, 24, 36–7
Samhain 48–9
Satan/Satanism 146, 164–5, 204, 207–11, 228, 248, 252–3
Sator (Rotas) square 184
Saturn 12–13, 135, 188–9
Scorpio 16, 18, 22, 24, 36–7
Seal of Solomon 68, 186, 193, 214, 239, 242
seals 186, 188–9
seasons 10, 36, 48–9, 52–5, 249
sefirot 131, 230–3, 239
Set (Seth) 22, 206–7, 248
shatkona 68, 240
sigils 186–7, 190–3, 211, 214, 243
silver 134–5, 140
snake 26–8, 55, 57, 58, 60, 71, 117, 240, 245
Solomon 186, 193, 204, 210, 212–13, 214, 220
Star of David 68, 193, 214, 239, 242
Stone Age 34–5, 152–3
Stonehenge 152–3, 160
suksma sharira 66–7
sulphur 133
Sun 10, 12–13, 24, 39, 101, 135, 188

T
taboo 34
t'ai 40
Taijitu 39
tantrism 156–7, 241
Tarot 163, 164, 194–8
Taurus 14–15, 18, 22, 24, 37
Temple of Set 248
tetractys 154
Theban alphabet 166–9
Thelema 230, 241, 246–7
Theosophical Society 228, 240–1
Third Eye 69
tiger 26–8, 42, 44, 111
tin 134–5
totem 34
Tree of Life 46–7, 99, 230–3, 239
trees 46–51, 93, 115
tria prima 133, 242
trigrams 38, 40–1
Trithemius, Johannes 164, 166–7, 170, 172
turtle 55, 62, 64, 110, 114
Tzolk'in 30–1

U
Uranus 12–13

V
Venus 10, 12–13, 135, 189
Virgo 16, 18, 22, 24, 37
Vodou vèvè 70–1
vulture 119

W
Wadjet 89, 246
Wicca 15, 49, 166, 228, 248, 250–1
wind 54–5, 117, 251
witchcraft 204, 250–1
wuxing 38–9

X
Xipe totec 75

Y
yantra 156, 158–9, 241
Yggdrasil 46–7
yin and yang 38–40, 207
Yule 46, 48–9

Z
zodiac 10, 14–31, 36, 42, 140
Zoroastrianism 206–7

ABOUT THE AUTHOR

Eric Chaline is an author and editor based in London. He has a special interest in religion and philosophy, especially in relation to East Asia, Mesoamerica and India. He has written books on a range of subjects, including history, travel, and health and fitness. His published works include *The Book of Zen*, *The Book of Gods and Goddesses*, *Simple Path to Yoga*, *101 Dilemmas for the Armchair Philosopher*, *Lost Treasures*, *History's Worst Inventions*, *Fifty Minerals that Changed the Course of History* and *Ancient Greece*.

IMAGE CREDITS